The Home Maker

The Home Maker

Elisha-Rei Jacobs

To order additional copies of this book, contact:
Xlibris
1-800-455-039
www.Xlibris.com.au
Orders@Xlibris.com.au
808200

CONTENTS

Foreword

As a minister of the Australian Christian Churches (Assembly Of God), Pastor Elisha-Rei Jacobs has been challenged by the increasing ills of Society destroying the home. The concern, borne out of his personal experience is prevalent in both the Country of Origin and his adopted one.

His passion for the word, love for Elohiym and Concern for broken homes inspired the writing of this book written from a Biblical Hebraic perspective.

The HOME MAKER is a first from this anointed teacher [LAMED/ MOWREH(למד מורה) who is evolving to be a Hebrew scholar.

I am indeed blessed to have been part of his ministry as Student, Colleague and Co-laborer Extra honor to be offered the space to write this [foreword.] I recommend the "THE HOME MAKER" to pastors who have concern for the restoration of Godly homes; parents who are presently caught in the discomfort of having to experience the traumas that come with dysfunctional homes, and a recommended read for aspiring home makers.

Early detection and management should restore homes and realign families back to their pre-ordained vocation and "THE HOME MAKER" is Elohiym's gift to this estranged world.

Jope Bainivalu (Rev.)
Founder "MIDWAY MINISTRY"
Helping Small Church Grow

Preface

Our local church in Sydney Australia committed and set as its mission, sending me to the islands of Fiji twice each year; teaching Biblical Hebrew to those that desire to learn. My July-August trip in 2016 presented a slightly different and busier schedule. Invited by one of the established denominations in Fiji AGOFI, (Apostle Gospel Outreach Fellowship International), to introduce Biblical Hebrew to their members. Whilst there, I was also asked to facilitate "streaming" for their 2016 National Conference. The week's program included an hour session on the Wednesday to hear presentations from the local police.

I heard the alarming and sad statistic; 95% of "rape and domestic violence in Fiji, are committed by "Christians" involving close family members. My mind has been occupied, and questions after questions I ask, why? And what can be done?

Upon returning the preoccupation was so much, and felt in my heart the desire to seek the Lord in His Word to answer these questions.

Being sixty one years old then, I believe I had done sufficient living to qualify my assertion. Looking at myself and where I am, I tried to ascertain the difference in the reason some are engaging in what I would not do in two life times. I found the upbringing was so crucial in my life, and when I hear or see behaviors contrary to what I was taught as morally right, I believe it is the upbringing, or the lack thereof, a contributing factor to the problem.

UpBringing

I am the sixth of seven children, (including a brother who died as a young boy). A school teacher in the late 1940's to early 1960's when remuneration is not as substantial, my father only had money for education to six children, and not much for anything else.

In my endeavor to collect as many verses, books and chapters pertaining to families and upbringing, I got to read Proverbs chapter thirty one. I realized that I knew this woman, in fact I lived with this woman.

Late fifties to early sixties three of my older siblings were working and the rest are still at home. She wakes up between four and five in the morning, to prepare breakfast and lunch for those who work, and those who were going to school. Once a week we might have bread with no butter for breakfast, considered a treat, otherwise our breakfast and lunch consist of what she produces from her plantation, they were delicious and healthy. As soon as breakfast is over, my mother and I were off to her plantation.

She did not teach me a lot by articulation, nor did I ask a lot of questions, but I believe; most of the lessons I learnt were through deeds not words, there was not so much theory, but practicality.

About four thirty in the afternoon, it was time to return home; dinner to be prepared and other chores attended to.

At dinner time my mother would pretend she is eating, but looking around to see if anyone wants seconds. Yours truly sitting next to her, never having to look, but she almost telepathically knew I would love seconds. I would have this surprise look on my face, seeing my plate is filled again. When I look at her, I see this smile reassuring me; "I got your back."

Sometimes after dinner, she would be siting at the corner of the kitchen after all the washing is done; having a cup of tea and a piece of cassava; that was her dinner because there was no more food left. Her face is still a display of joy and satisfaction; a feeling I get to experience years later; when I cook at home and my son would say to me; "dad that was nice, can I have some more?"

Though my father was the disciplinarian; for me most of life's lesson was taught by my mother, not so much by what she tells me, but by the way she conducts herself around people, the way she handles confrontational situations.

Living in a communal set up, requires respect and recognition of hierarchical standings and status. Most importantly, to have respect for other people and things that belong to them. She also emphasized the importance of forgiveness.

I believe the undeniable bond between a child and a mother, can only be explained by a mother. A bond that begins nine months earlier, and continued through childhood.

For a mother to carry out her duties to her children and her husband like the way my mother did; her inspiration had to come from within where God speaks; complemented by her willingness to obey. This book is dedicated to the memory of my mother;

Irinieta Bale Modrau

Introduction

Every government in the entire world knows that the only way to correct society, is the restoration of homes, more precisely families. The issue of poverty is rife in the majority of places, especially, third world countries. The United Nation sustainable goals writes: *"Extreme poverty rates have been cut by more than half since 1990. While this is a remarkable achievement, one in five people in developing regions still live on less than $1.25 a day, and there are millions more who make little more than this daily amount, plus many people risk slipping back into poverty. Poverty is more than the lack of in-come and resources to ensure a sustainable livelihood. Its manifestations include hunger and malnutrition, limited access to education and other basic services, social discrimination and exclusion as well as the lack of participation in decision-making. Economic growth must be inclusive to provide sustainable jobs and promote equality."*

Governments are also concerned in the violation of our civil laws as well as moral laws. There is an alarming increase in the number of killings, divorce, and general criminal activities. An interesting statistic reveals that countries with worse criminal records are those that embrace Christianity as the preferred religion.

The country of Honduras for example; with a population of 8.2 million (estimation 1ˢᵗ January 2016), has the highest criminality rate of 90 homicides per 100,000 people. Approximately 86% are Catholic and evangelical Christians.

Sad to notice that the very people that have the opportunity and access to the blueprint of home building, are those guilty of violating them.

This book is expected to generate controversy, depending on the basis with which one adjudicates from; human rights, equal rights, gender equality to name a few. The intention is nowhere near those assumptions; rather; they are the basis that I believe brought about the dismantling of homes. We look at women's right, from our own perspectives, but ignore women's right according to the Word of God.

This book is meant to empower women around the world. For so long; religion and culture have belittled women's role in our society. To some extent, they are referred to as the weaker gender.

The information you find in this book comes from observing the text of the bible from an Hebraic perspective.

I believe the answer for our society to at least have a chance of regaining integrity and revisiting the meaning of life, is in the rebuilding of homes more than the construction of housing schemes. For this to happen we need to identify "the home maker."

Right now if you believe in God, you would be saying; he is the home maker: No; he is not the home maker, rather he is the initiator of homes.

Elohim created everything to initiate what I believe, is paramount to the design he has put in place regarding the family; **when our children leave the House, they will take with them the Home.** Whatever they learn in the homes; they will take with them.

The home is made up of numerous components; mother, father, children, house, food, work, values, religions, belief, etc.

To start, one needs to go back to the scriptures for authentication. We ask ourselves the question; Is the home important to Elohim? Before answering the question, a certainty must be revealed; **God has to build the house.**

Note: Hebrew is written and read from right to left.

Chapter One

The House and The Home

Earlier we mentioned; what I believe sets the central message of this book: "the children leave the HOUSE, but take the HOME with them." Though a lot will be written about the home in this book, but one cannot ignore the importance of the house. One can have all the ingredients, and the knowledge to make a cake; without an oven, every effort is futile.

Isaiah 66:1King James Version (KJV)
Thus saith the Lord, The heaven is my throne, and the earth is my footstool: where is the house that ye build (תבנו tib̲nûw) unto me? and where is the place of my rest?

I want to draw our attention to the verb and to whom the question is intended.

תבנו *tib̲nûw* - this word is a conjugation of the Hebrew word בנה *bānāh* meaning to build, or more appropriately in the Hebrew grammatical structure, often articulated in the 3msg. (3rd person masculine singular past tense), "he built." however the addition of the "pronominal suffix" ו changes the number and gender to 2mpl, (2nd person masculin plural). Prefixed with ת determining tense, in what is called the "yiqtol form," brings the future tense: "you shall build."

The house is built first and foremost for the dwelling place of Elohim. The man and the woman need to understand before ever thinking of starting a home, they both need to be firmly founded on the word of God. In a latter chapter we shall discuss about the marriage counsellor, and the importance of their impartation.

I applaud the effort of people who have written excellent literature based on facts and data from real life occurrences. Unfortunately these are symptoms we are trying to correct and not the root.

Example: marriage counsellors suggesting the couple live together first on a trial bases, after years of evil consummation decide whether they should be married or not.

We ignore the blue print of marriage, (the word of God) to the extent we now are faced with ungodly union as an accepted norm.

Building a House.

Proverbs 24:3-4 King James Version (KJV)
3 Through wisdom is an house builded; and by understanding it is established: 4 And by knowledge shall the chambers be filled with all precious and pleasant riches.

The three things instrumental in the building of the house are:

1. Wisdom - builds the house (only the creator can give wisdom).
2. Understanding - establishes (making decision according to the blue print—Word of God).
3. Knowledge - furnishes (knowledge of the blue print—The Word of God).

Psalm 127:1 King James Version (KJV)
127 Except the Lord build the house, they labour in vain that build it: except the Lord keep the city, the watchman waketh but in vain.

Adonai (the Lord) will give you wisdom if you ask him.

James 1:5King James Version (KJV)
5 If any of you lack wisdom, let him ask of God, that giveth to all men liberally, and upbraided not; and it shall be given him.

Ask the Lord also for understanding and knowledge.

Proverbs 2:6King James Version (KJV)
6 For the Lord giveth wisdom: out of his mouth cometh knowledge and understanding.

The Home Inside the House

Deuteronomy 21:12King James Version (KJV) *12 Then thou shalt bring her home* תוך *tavek to thine house,* בית *bayit and she shall shave her head, and pare her nails;*

Joshua 2:18King James Version (KJV) 18 *Behold, when we come in-to the land, thou shalt bind this line of scarlet thread in the window which thou didst let us down by: and thou shalt bring thy father, and thy mother, and thy brethren, and all thy father's household,*(בית *bayit) home (*הביתה *habāyitah) unto thee*

Elohim (God) to build the house:
The effort of making the home will and only succeed when Adonay/ Elohim builds the house.

Psalm 127:1King James Version (KJV) *Except the Lord build the house, they labour in vain that build it: except the Lord keep the city, the watchman waketh but in vain.*

Suffice to mention, and may also be a warning the opposition to Elohiym building the house is one founded on the "pattern of this world," and not the foundation of Yeshua Mashiach (Jesus Christ).

Romans 12:2King James Version (KJV) *2 And be not conformed to this world: but be ye transformed by the renewing of your mind, that ye may prove what is that good, and acceptable, and perfect, will of God.*

One asks the question; how will Elohiym build the house? The answer is found in Proverbs twenty four.

Proverbs 24:3-4King James Version (KJV) *3 Through wisdom is an house builded; and by understanding it is established: 4 And by knowledge shall the chambers be filled with all precious and pleasant riches.*

Three main components founded on the Word of God.

1. Wisdom builds
2. Understanding establishes
3. Knowledge furnishes

Unless the husband and the wife understands this principles; we will build in vain.

The foundation is and will always be Yeshua Messiah.
1 Corinthians 3:11King James Version (KJV) **11 For other foundation can no man lay than that is laid, which is Jesus Christ.**

Wisdom: חכמה transliterated, *chokmah*. A derivative of the Hebrew root word חכם chakam meaning to be wise in mind, words, and action. Only God can give wisdom when you ask him.

James 1:5King James Version (KJV) 5 **If any of you lack wisdom, let him ask of God, that giveth to all men liberally, and upbraideth not; and it shall be given him.**

Wisdom's impartation is always accompanied by knowledge and understanding using the Spirit of God.

Exodus 31:3King James Version (KJV) 3 *And I have filled him with the spirit of God, in wisdom, and in understanding, and in knowledge, and in all manner of workmanship,*

He used ordinary people in all manner of workmanship. Exodus chapter thirty-five in particular; when he picked Bezaleel, a man with no formal training, to do all manner of workmanship. (verse thirty one).

When Elohiym is invited and allowed to build the house, he will give and teach you the know how through his Holy Spirit. There is no excuse and great hope is available as he builds our minds, our words and our actions through the strengthening and leading of the Holy Spirit.

Understanding: תבונה *tabôwnah* meaning discretion, reason, the contrast of foolishness.

    a. **A person of understanding is slow to wrath** Proverbs 14:29King James Version (KJV) *29 He that is slow to wrath is of great understanding: ...* (תבונה *tabownah*)

    b. **And walks uprightly** Proverbs 15:21King James Version (KJV) *21 Folly is joy to him that is destitute of wisdom: but a man of understanding* (תבונה *tabôwnah*) *walketh uprightly.*

תבונה *tabôwnah* comes from the root word בין *biyn* means to separate mentally. To pay attention, to be intelligent, perceive, prudent, give understanding, to teach. Looks like understanding is the separation of the "big picture," and the "finer details" of accomplishing a goal. I suggest that we are talking about the different functions of the left and right hemispheres of our brains; thus the meaning of "biyn," as to separate mentally.

Knowledge: דעת da‘ath a feminine noun meaning knowledge, knowing, learning, discern., to be aware. Another Hebrew root word ידע *yāda‘* meaning to know, skilful. To know relationally, or experientially.

The Only Thing We Own

How many people know that the only thing we own is our "choice," God gave us the freedom to **choose**. We say we own land, house and material things, when we are mere custodians. Tell me what you take; that you supposedly own, when the breath you do not own is taken by the owner?

Psalm 24:1King James Version (KJV) *The earth is the Lord's, and the fulness thereof; the world, and they that dwell therein.*

It is God's will for us to be successful in this life; and to be good stewards of all that he blessed us with. However there is not enough room in your coffin for the money and the house and all the property; one only takes the consequences of one's choice. We all are going to be judged according to the choices we make in this life.

Job 1:21King James Version (KJV)
21 And said, Naked came I out of my mother's womb, and naked shall I return thither: the Lord gave, and the Lord hath taken away; blessed be the name of the Lord.

Suggestion to what we choose:
King Solomon chose an "understanding heart" when asked by God of what he wanted. He chose wisdom and understanding.

1 Kings 3:12King James Version (KJV) *12 Behold, I have done according to thy words: lo, I have given thee a wise and an understanding heart; so that there was none like thee before thee, neither after thee shall any arise like unto thee.*

God has also given us options, and we are to make choices. He is urging us to choose "life."

Deuteronomy 30:19King James Version (KJV) *19 I call heaven and earth to record this day against you, that I have set before you life (*חיים

chayyim) *and death, blessing and cursing: therefore choose life,* (חיים chayyim) *that both thou and thy seed may live:*

What Life is he offering?: Life mentioned in Deuteronomy above; can be misconstrued with the normal day to day existence. To begin; one needs to go back to the beginning to make sense of the end. (Isaiah 46:10).

Genesis 2:7King James Version (KJV) *7 And the Lord God formed man of the dust of the ground, and breathed into his nostrils the breath of life;* (חיים chayyim) *and man became a living soul.*

When God breath life into man for the first time in Genesis 2:7; man was filled with love, joy prosperity, wisdom, and kindness. God was saying to the Israelites, and saying to us now to choose that life.

Notice the Hebrew word used in both verses is (חיים chayyim), a derivative of the Hebrew root word (חיה chayah) meaning to revive, make alive, keep alive. This was the pre-fall life filled with righteousness, holiness, wisdom and kindness.

The same is before us to choose. Through the eyes of God we will see our destiny and the maintenance of the road toward it when we attain the life on offer; one and the same as Yeshua Mashiach, our Lord and Saviour.

John 14:6King James Version (KJV) 6 Jesus saith unto him, I am the way, the truth, and the life: no man cometh unto the Father, but by me.

SUMMARY

The house is essentially built with divine attributes from God, he gives wisdom, understanding and knowledge. I suggest the word of God; (scriptures) will supply the blueprint, to provide the basis with which the "home" will be shaped.

A section that will be covered later emphasizes the importance of marriage counseling. Courtship is where the tone is set for a Godly relationship.

Chapter Two

First Letter of The First Word in The Bible

The Home is Important to Elohiym (God)

I want to introduce to us the very first phrase in the bible. Genesis 1:1 King James Version (KJV) ***In the beginning ...***

In the beginning, is the translation of one Hebrew word; בראשית transliterated, **bᵉrēshiyth**

Let me draw your attention to the first letter; ב This letter is named "bayit" which is Hebrew for house or family. This is indicative of how important a family is to Elohiym. The Hebrew letter בbet; is used as a prepositional prefix "in" to the Hebrew word ראשית rēshîyth, meaning; "beginning." thus the phrase, "In the beginning." The beginning of the nation of Israel, is the family of Jacob.

Now that we have established what I suggest is the first thing that comes out of his word; it is time to start working our way to finding who the "home maker" is.

The components of home as mentioned before;

- Father (male)

- Mother (female)
- Offsprings

Parenting

This is a subject of discussion at different levels of governance now days. The gender of parenthood is at the centre, where the notions of same gender parents were to be accepted in our society. Lawmakers differ in their opinions; sadly in some cases, lawmakers have become lawbreakers. They break the very law that governs our existence to satisfy their own dark agenda.

At this point I want to introduce a scripture that stipulates the law our legislators are trying to break, if not already broken.

Genesis 1:27King James Version (KJV) *27 So God created (ויברא man in his own image, in the image of God created (ברא he him; male and female created (ברא he them.*

Notice the word "created" used three times, with past tense. One of the unique characteristic of the Hebrew language; is the ability to record a current event, and by inflection transform the same word to effect the future.

ברא this is the Hebrew root word transliterated; "bārā' meaning to create, translated **"he created"** in the King James Version. This would be in the Qal Qatal form normally articulated in the "third person masculine singular past tense," (3msg past tense) **"he created."**

ויברא In this conjugation of the same word; ברא the addition of the letters'ו as prefix, changes the tense into continuous, so it reads; "and he is creating," thus indicating the delivery of the creation of human is a continuing process, Suffice to mention, it is not the evolution, but the delivery of the same that was spoken.

But the creation of "male and female," is a one-time event; spoken in the "Qal Qatal" form meaning either a male or a female suggesting there is no in between.

This component of the family will not change, however hard some may try to justify their own individual agenda, it will only prove that they are trying to legalize a morally illegal and ungodly union. Should we legalize the wishes of these minorities? God forbid! The family unit could one day see the possibility of having more than one woman as wives to one man, living as a family, when polygamy is legalized. A relationship currently in existence with animal, not human.

Male And Female

The comments above warrants a proper look into the verse, to determine what the bible says about "**male and female**." Genesis 1:27King James Version (KJV) **27** *So God created man in his own image, in the image of God created he him;* ***male and female*** *created he them.*

Male: Translated from the Hebrew word זכר *zākār*
Female: Translated from the Hebrew word נקבה **n**ᵉ*qābah*

Qualification to be female.

In a homosexual affair the males have to decide who is to be the female in the relationship.

The argument of female can be solved by understanding who is qualified by observing the following scripture.

Genesis 3:16King James Version (KJV)

16 Unto the woman he said, I will greatly multiply thy sorrow and thy conception; in sorrow **_thou shalt bring forth_** *; (*תלדי *children and thy desire shall be to thy husband, and he shall rule over thee.*

This verse offers so much to support the qualification criteria of a female. We focus closely on the phrase; ***thou shalt bring forth***. The Hebrew text; תלדי transliterated ***tēldiy*** is the conjugation of the Hebrew root word ילד ***yalad*** meaning to "bear children."

The addition of the prefix ת did two things: changes the tense to present and future, thus the phrase; "thou shall." Secondly, because yod י, is a weak letter, while it is the first letter in the Qal stem ילד ***yalad***, when conjugated to the "Yiqtol verbal stem, it disappears altogether. The letter ת at the end indicates to us the gender of the subject as second person feminine singular (2fsg).

Unless one can naturally conceive and bring forth a child, one cannot be female. The female must have desire for only one individual male; the husband.

Leviticus 12:2King James Version (KJV) …*If a woman have conceived seed, and born a **man child**: (זכר zakar) then she shall be unclean seven days; according to the days of the separation for her infirmity shall she be unclean.*

Leviticus 12:5King James Version (KJV) *5 But if she bear a **maid child**, (נקבה n͟eqābah) then she shall be unclean two weeks, as in her separation: and she shall continue in the blood of her purifying threescore and six days.*

The gender verification determines the length of the woman's purifying period. One week if the child is a boy and two weeks if the child was a girl. However it is important to note that the woman not the man conceived and gave birth.

Consolidating the point that female naturally conceive and bring forth a child.

Male: זכר *zakār*

This word is a derivation of the Hebrew root זכר zākar. It means to remember, to mark (so as to be recognized).

Why would the creator of the human body use this particular word to identify a male? I suggest the offspring of a home is remembered, marked and recognized by the Father's DNA.

Female: נקבה *n*ᵉ*qābah*

Comes from the Hebrew root; נקב nāqāb̲ meaning to puncture, to pierce, perforate. The feminine noun נקבה *n*ᵉ*qābah* means female, sometimes referred to as woman, also reference to one that has a hole. Thus the word נקבה *n*ᵉ*qābah* female is also used for animals.

Romans 1:27 King James Version (KJV) *27 And likewise also the men, leaving the natural use of the woman, burned in their lust one toward another; men with men working that which is unseemly, and receiving in themselves that recompence of their error which was meet.*

Elohiym's (God's) intention creating male and female was for procreation purposes when he commanded "they multiply." When they disobeyed him, eating from the tree of the knowledge of good and evil; not only did their eyes open; they also knew they were naked and decided to cover their nakedness because it was shameful to be exposed.

Since then, what was supposed to be for procreation purposes becomes the tool of lust, and sadly most marriages are based on lust not love.

Genesis 3:7 King James Version (KJV) *7 And the eyes of them both were opened, and they knew that they were naked; and they sewed fig leaves together, and made themselves aprons.*

The verse specifically mentioned that both their eyes were opened. They realized their nakedness and covered themselves with leaves. Another aspect would be their consciousness of flesh that generates not only the lust of the flesh also the lust of the eye.

1 John 2:16King James Version (KJV) *16 For all that is in the world, the lust of the flesh, and the lust of the eyes, and the pride of life, is not of the Father, but is of the world.*

Special Mention:

Before leaving this chapter, may I elaborate a little on what we alluded to in the introduction, regarding human rights, against our God-given right.

All we do and say are qualified against only two measurements;

1.   The word of God and
2.   The pattern of the world.

Romans 12:2King James Version (KJV) *2 And be not conformed to this world: but be ye transformed by the renewing of your mind, that ye may prove what is that good, and acceptable, and perfect, will of God.*

Gay Rights

God created male and female, there is no confusion except the choices we make in our minds. Homosexuality, alcoholism and in fact all behavioral patterns are products of abuse or otherwise in family upbringing that the children are exposed to.

The pattern of the world is saying; "These men were born gay, not made gay, and their sexuality is a gift from God, not the result of sexual abuse. Plus, there are plenty of gay men who were never abused and plenty of straight men who were abused as boys and never turned gay."

The word of God says:

Psalm 139:14King James Version (KJV) *14 I will praise thee; for I am fearfully (*נוראות **nôrā'owth***) and wonderfully made: marvellous are thy works; and that my soul knoweth right well.*

נוראות **nôrā'owth** is translated **as "fearfully,"** the word is a conjugation of the Hebrew root word ירא **yāre'** meaning fear. The word is further inflected in the "niphal" stem, thus the prefix **"נ"** suggesting a reflexive voice. We then can deduce that the subject, or the potter in this instance, takes great care in fear of breaking the clay.

Isaiah 64:8King James Version (KJV) *8 But now, O Lord, thou art our father; we are the clay, and thou our potter; and we all are the work of thy hand.*

Dr. Michael Brown author of: *Outlasting the Gay Revolution and Where Homosexual Activism Is Really Going and How to Turn the Tide* wrote:

"As for the notion that people are born gay, not only would that suggest that infants can relate to the concepts of sexual and romantic attraction (which they obviously cannot), but it would also ignore the fact that our upbringing and environment have profound effects on us. Why deny such an obvious reality?"

Women's Right

They fight for equality, when the word of God already suggest, male and female are equal. I believe "women's right" activists unknowingly, further exacerbates the narrative already exist in our society that women are a weaker gender.

Clarification in chapter five, "Elohim the Initiator."

Planned Parenthood

"To the world, I am an attorney who had an abortion, and, to myself, I am an attorney because I had an abortion."

Words of Janice Mac Avoy, pro parenthood. (refer Ref)

Women's right's demand for equality has escalated to murdering a child in abortion.

SUMMARY

When we deviate from the Word of God, Satan plays with our minds by twisting the word of God to suit what we perceive in Satan's insistence as our right.

Paul perfectly surmise in Romans chapter one.

Romans 1:24-25Complete Jewish Bible (CJB) *24 This is why God has given them up to the vileness of their hearts' lusts, to the shameful misuse of each other's bodies. 25 They have exchanged the truth of God for falsehood, by worshipping and serving created things, rather than the Creator — praised be he for ever. Amen.*

Chapter Three

What The Scriptures say about Women

There is always differences in opinion in whether Adam was created first before Eve, or should Eve be talking to the serpent, when the instructions; "not to eat of the tree of knowledge of good and evil," was given to Adam.

The assumption that the woman was created after Adam, sometimes leads to men thinking they are boss; true or not depends on how we perceive the scriptures. We begin by forensically investigating Genesis 5:2

Genesis 5:2King James Version (KJV)
2 Male and female created he them; and blessed them, and called their name Adam, in the day when they were created.

Consider the phrase; "called their name Adam." if you are reading the same bible, this is not a misprint, but a further indication that Elohim (God) was talking about human. The word Adam, is translated from the Hebrew word אדם ʾādām. Adam is not the word man, but Hebrew word for "human being."

In the day when they were created is a reference to Genesis chapter one verse twenty seven. (Gen 1:27)

Genesis 1:27King James Version (KJV)
27 So God created man in his own image, in the image of God created he him; male and female created he them.

According to Genesis 5:2, the name Adam is both for male and female. The word Adam even though translated as man; is "human." Notice the pronoun, "them" is in both verses; I suggest that when Adam was uttered by Elohim, both the man and the woman were spoken into existence. Reminds me of a verse we later will discuss;

Genesis 2:23King James Version (KJV) *23 And Adam said, This is now bone of my bones, and flesh of my flesh: she shall be called Woman, because she was taken out of Man.*

The woman was taken out of man; but to further consolidate the point, we go to a verse earlier than that:

Genesis 2:22King James Version (KJV) *22 And the rib, which the Lord God had taken from man, **made** he a woman, and brought her unto the man.*

Woman was built not made.

The keyword in this verse is **made**. The word for made in He-brew is עשׂה transliterated ʿāsāh. The same word used in Genesis 1:26; "**Let us "make" man**…" May I remind us that we were made from things not seen. What would that be? I suggest we were made by the unseen word of Elohim. For example; if someone is talking to you, you can hear what is said, but you cannot see the word.

Hebrews 11:3King James Version (KJV) *3 Through faith we under-stand that the worlds were framed by the word of God, so that things which are seen were not made of things which do appear.*

But the word made, used in Genesis chapter two verse twenty two is translated from the Hebrew word; בנה transliterated bānāh, meaning to build. Eve was not made, she was built. Notice the woman was not made from an unseen thing, but built from the raw material already available, i.e. the rib taken from the man's side. Could I suggest that God packed X chromosomes into the bone (rib) and built the woman?

Weaker Gender

As mentioned earlier, our cultures and religion sometimes refer to women as the "weaker gender." Women are brainwashed to the point when confronted with threatening situation, offer less resistance because they have been inculcated with the message of weakness. I do not believe for a moment that women are weak; their strength is the same as man if not more.

Submission verses Weakness:

Ephesians 5:22King James Version (KJV) *22 Wives, submit your-selves unto your own husbands, as unto the Lord.*

We have erroneously misinterpreted this verse, to authenticate our claim and perception of women to be the weaker gender. Let us see what Elohim said in regard to this from the beginning. **Genesis 3:16King James Version (KJV)** *16 Unto the woman he said, I will greatly multiply thy sorrow and thy conception; in sorrow thou shalt bring forth children; and thy desire shall be to thy husband, and **he shall rule over thee**.* (ימשל yimshal)

ימשל yimshal comes from the root word משל mashal meaning to rule, to reign, to govern in leadership not in compulsion. Some people may liken this to a slave master. Another verse used this verb but it meant something else.

Job 41:33King James Version (KJV) *33 Upon earth there is not his like,* (משל mashal) *who is made without fear.*

I suggest that man was to rule in leadership of someone like him.

Submit

The phrase "submit yourself," is translated from the Hebrew word; **התעני** hith'āniy. The verb central to this word **עני** 'āniy comes from the Hebrew root word **ענה** 'ānah meaning "he humbled." The root is conjugated further with what is called in Hebrew grammatical structure a verbal stem, "hithpael." It causes a reflexive effect, where the subject is also the object of the action. The woman described herself in Proverbs 31: 11; as her husband's property; therefore he can trust her. Thus my suggestion that the humbling is not by compulsion but out of fortitude. It takes a strong person to do that, wives humble yourselves; Ephesians 5:22. Hopefully you will view this verse differently next you read it.

Women are strong

First we look at the application of the Hebraic verses to determine what the bible says. We use the following verse.

Genesis 2:23King James Version (KJV) *23 And Adam said, This is now bone of my bones, and flesh of my flesh: she shall be called Woman, because she was taken out of Man.*

"Bone of my bones" is the translation of the Hebrew phrase: **עצם מעצמי** transliterated; 'etsem mē'etsāmay. There are four different levels of interpretation of scriptures in Hebrew.

Level One עשׁט-pashat : This is a root word means; to spread

out, to strip, to unclothe, to open. Means the first and obvious meaning.

Level Two רמשׁ ramas Primitive Hebrew root word, it means to crawl or move with shot steps. The word was used in Genesis 1:26 when describing "creeping things."

Genesis 1:26King James Version (KJV) *26 And God said, Let us make man in our image, after our likeness: and let them have do-minion over the fish of the sea, and over the fowl of the air, and over the cattle, and over all the earth, and over every creeping thing that creepeth* (רמש ramas) *upon the earth.*

The small steps from פשט- pashat revealing another meaning.

Level Three דרש-darash means to frequent, to follow, search, inquire, make inquisition, to pursue, seek and ask.

Psalm 24:6King James Version (KJV) 6 This is the generation of them that seek (-דרשdarash) him, that seek (דרש- **darash**) thy face, O Jacob. Selah.

Level Four: דוֹס **sowd**

Confidentiality is in the heart of the term. Job used this term to refer to his close friendship with God.

Job 29:4King James Version (KJV) *4 As I was in the days of my youth, when the secret* (סוד **sowd**) *of God was upon my tabernacle;*

Elohim establishes a close, intimate relationship with those who revere him and walk uprightly.

When Adam called the woman; "bone of my bones," in the פשט- pashat level, it meant just that, but in the סוד **sowd** level the word bone is translated from the Hebrew word עצם‘etsem. This word also means "strength." Therefore Adam was also saying to the woman: "strength of my strength," or at least he is saying; "your strength is the same as that of my strength." I prefer to think that Adam is saying to the woman; "when you are strong, I am strong."

If that is not convincing enough; let us look at the words spoken when Elohim suggested he made the man a "help meet."

The verse is found in Genesis 2:18

When Elohim decided the idea of bringing man and woman together, he did not say, "I am going to bring him a wife," nor did he say, "I will bring him a mother, he said "I am going to make him a help meet."

Genesis 2:18King James Version (KJV)
*18 And the Lord God said, It is not good that the man should be alone; I will make him an **help meet** for him*

The phrase **"help meet"** translated from the Hebrew text as: עזר נגדו transliterated as ʿēzer negāduw

עזר ʿēzer translated as help. Derivative of the verb עזר ʿāzar, meaning to surround, to protect, to aid. I suggest that the woman according to עזר ʿāzār is assigned to surround and protect the husband. In case one has not seen what a body guard looks like; they are strong and fearless. Also the reason a bride walks around the groom seven times in some Jewish wedding, before the ceremony starts.

Brings to mind the question, why the serpent went to the woman and not the man? Though you may not agree because it is only my opinion, I suggest Satan knew if he can weaken the bodyguard, the man is easy target.

נגדו negāduw means to be in front or before him looking back. Also means directly opposite. The woman is in front of the man facing him. Not forward to lead but looking backward to communicate and receive direction from the man.

It is not about authority, but working in harmony according to their God given ability.

I can hear questions being asked: what if the man is not there? Listen to Adam's declaration: strength of my strength, that is what Elohim created women to be; equal strength if not more than man. I urge the women of the world not look down on themselves, but believe in the GOD that created this great big world and enough space for them to express their God-given ability and responsibility according to the blueprint he has provided.

Why did God order the wife to submit to the husband? Using two verses from the bible to clarify the word submit.

1. **Ephesians 5:22 King James Version (KJV)** *22 Wives, <u>submit yourselves.</u>(התעני **hith͑aniy**) unto your own husbands, as unto the Lord.*
2. **Genesis 16:9 King James Version (KJV)** *9 And the angel of the Lord said unto her, Return to thy mistress, and <u>submit thyself</u> (התעני **hith͑aniy**) under her hands.*

התעני **hith͑aniy** is from the Hebrew word ענה **͑ānah** meaning to abase self or humble. The word is further conjugated in the Hebrew verbal stem; "hithpael." The Hithpael Stem can be used to express an intensive type of action with a reflexive voice. The reflexive voice is used when the subject of the verb performs the verbal action upon itself.

It takes courage and strength to abase oneself. In Ephesians 5:22 women are ordered to submit not by compulsion, but because of design and fortitude, and that is strength.

I believe God has equipped women with the ability and the passion to handle situations when things do not turn out as expected. Think of the many mothers that had to raise, teach and discipline children because the man had left for some reason.

Remember the words the male (Adam) said; "bones of my bones" or **"strength of my strength."**

Somehow men have this unconscious tendency to pile unwanted chores on women, and particularly Abraham asked Sarai to lie for him.

Sarai

Abraham fearing for his life; ask his wife Sarai to lie for him.

Genesis 12:10-12King James Version (KJV) *10 And there was a famine in the land: and Abram went down into Egypt to sojourn there; for the famine was grievous in the land. 11 And it came to pass, when he was come near to enter into Egypt, that he said unto Sarai his wife, Behold now, I know that thou art a fair woman to look upon:*

12 Therefore it shall come to pass, when the Egyptians shall see thee, that they shall say, This is his wife: and they will kill me, but they will save thee alive.

I am in no way encouraging man to ask their wives to lie, but how many times do men leave children home with their wives, and pursue interests of their own.

Nowhere did I see Sarai kicking and screaming when she was led away; because she was doing her duty of protecting the husband.

Eve

Adam, when confronted for eating from the forbidden tree; quickly blamed the woman.

Genesis 3:12King James Version (KJV) *12 And the man said, The woman whom thou gavest to be with me, she gave me of the tree, and I did eat.*

Other examples in the bible will further illustrate the relationship between the church and Messiah.

Yeshua qualified the power and strength of the church claiming the gates of hell will not prevail against it.

Matthew 16:18King James Version (KJV) *18 And I say also unto thee, That thou art Peter, and upon this rock I will build my church; and the gates of hell shall not prevail against it.*

Considering the church as the bride of Christ, Yeshua confirmed the strength and temerity on its role prescribed in the scriptures.

Chapter Four

The Man

Let me apologize in advance to those that might be offended with the terms used in this chapter. 'Man has three main tasks that heads the list of his priority:

a. Please God (fulfilling the will of God)
b. Provide for his family. (eat from the sweat of his brow).
c. Institute and establish a sincere and faith-filled atmosphere in the home, to facilitate moral and spiritual provision.

Let us look at the Hebrew words used for man/husband. The two words commonly used in the scriptures for husband or man, are:

1. אִישׁ transliterated ʾiysh. A man or an individual. It is also used to mean male or husband. This word does not indicate human kind, but male gender in particular. Hosea used the word to describe Elohim's special relationship to Israel.
    Hosea 2:16King James Version (KJV) *16 And it shall be at that day, saith the Lord, that thou shalt call me Ishi; and shalt call me no more Baali.*
2. אֱנוֹשׁ **transliterated** ʾenowsh meaning mortal. A derivative of the root word אָנַשׁ transliterated ʾānāsh meaning to be frail, feeble.

A word used also as man, but the application is for both male and female.

1. אדם transliterated ʾādam meaning "human being." Growing up, I always assume that Adam is male.

Genesis 5:2King James Version (KJV) *2 Male and female cre-ated he them; and blessed them, and called their name Adam, in the day when they were created*

When God built the "help meet," she was going to protect the frailty of the husband and the weaknesses of his ways. A woman that understands her role scripturally will recognize that she is there to strengthen the man. The scripture says that man shall leave his father and mother and cling to the wife and become one, not the other way around.

Matthew 19:5King James Version (KJV) ***5 And said, For this cause shall a man leave father and mother, and shall cleave to his wife: and they twain shall be one flesh?***

Interesting to read verse four where Yeshua (Jesus) mentioned: "***he which made them at the beginning made them male and female,*** "

Matthew 19:4King James Version (KJV)
4 And he answered and said unto them, Have ye not read, that he which made them at the beginning made them male and female. Yeshua himself confirmed that male and female according to him that created them.

The Man Sits at the Gate *Planner and Provider*

The gate is a place of thinkers, they calculate costs. The word gate comes the Hebrew word שער shaʿar. This word means to set a price. A miser

Proverbs 23:7King James Version (KJV) *7 For as he thinketh (*שער **shaʿar***) in his heart, so is he: Eat and drink, saith he to thee; but his heart is not with thee*

שׁער sha‘ar this Hebrew is translated "thinketh," means calculates. in the context of this verse is that of a miser, who counts the cost of everything their guests eat and drink. they find no enjoyments in the guests, all they worry about is the cost.

The man is a wise spender, never foolishly let go of hard earned money because he is always looking at the future of his generation.

Genesis 30:30King James Version (KJV)

30 For it was little which thou hadst before I came, and it is now increased unto a multitude; and the Lord hath blessed thee since my coming: and now when shall I provide for mine own house also?

Jacob pleading with his father-in-law to let him go so that he can provide for his family. Somehow he realized even though he is working hard, he is providing first for his father-in-law, then his family. He wanted to make his family his priority.

Endurance

When Elohim judged the man after eating from the tree of the knowledge of good and evil, he said to him in Genesis 3:17c .... *in sorrow shalt thou eat of it all the days of thy life;*

The word sorrow interestingly, translated from the Hebrew word עצבון transliterated ‘*etsāb̲own*. Comes from the Hebrew root word עצב ‘*ātsab̲.* There are two meanings for this word; the first is sorrow, pain, to grief, to shape, to fashion. Physical pain as described in Ecclesiastes chapter ten.

Ecclesiastes 10:9King James Version (KJV) *9 Whoso removeth stones shall be hurt (עצב‘ātsab̲) therewith; and he that cleaveth wood shall be endangered thereby.*

The word is used for woman too, she would have pain and toil during childbirth.

Genesis 3:16King James Version (KJV) *16 Unto the woman he said, I will greatly multiply thy sorrow (עֶצֶב‎ʿātsab) and thy conception; in sorrow thou shalt bring forth children; and thy desire shall be to thy husband, and he shall rule over thee.*

To the man God stated that he would have pain and grief working the ground to produce food.

Genesis 3:17b King James Version (KJV)*...Thou shalt not eat of it: cursed is the ground for thy sake; in sorrow עֶצֶב‎ʿātsab) shalt thou eat of it all the days of thy life;*

Comforted by the truth:

In our pain we get confidence and comfort, by understanding that, the initiator of the activities is our creator.

Genesis 5:29King James Version (KJV) *29 And he called his name Noah, saying, This same shall comfort us concerning our work and toil of our hands, because of the ground which the Lord hath cursed*

Interestingly the name "Noah" means to console, to comfort knowing that pain and sorrow is dealt with by embracing the truth.

Being a man; if given a choice between toiling the land for food, and the pain of childbirth, you know which would I choose; what is your choice?

Create activities for the home.

The second meaning generally refers to creative activity, such as the kind God exercised when he created the human body.

Job 10:8King James Version (KJV) *8 Thine hands have made me and fashioned* (עצבון *ʿetsābown*) *me together round about; yet thou dost destroy me.*

Also creative activity of people as suggested in Jeremiah 44:19,.

In both these instances, the word occurs in parallel to the word עשה *ʿāsāh* meaning to make or to do. The man is tasked to make the home an attractive place to go to.

The Disciplinarian

Deuteronomy 6:7King James Version (KJV)
7 And thou shalt teach them diligently unto thy children, and shalt talk of them when thou sittest in thine house, and when thou walkest by the way, and when thou liest down, and when thou risest up.

Proverbs 19:18King James Version (KJV) *18 <u>Chasten</u> (יסר yasar) <u>thy son</u> (בנך binka) while there is hope, and let not thy soul spare for his crying.*

יסר yasar means discipline
בנך binka translated "thy son."

These two Hebrew words explain the action of discipline through the Hebrew word יסר yasar. בנך binka supplies the object, the son, translated from the Hebrew word בן ben. The pronoun suffix ך ka supplies the subject as 2msg (2nd person masculine singular: YOU).

It is the duty of man according to the scriptures to discipline. All the activities listed above are ones that take place at home. How many fathers do we know, are relying on the elders and the pastors of the church to teach their children. The church is the place of congregational worship, fellowship and sharing; but the home is where they are taught. Parents, especially the father, should revisit responsibilities regarding the teaching of God's word. One cannot teach what they do not have.

Deuteronomy 6:6King James Version (KJV) *6 And these words, which
I command thee this day, shall be in thine heart:*

The man, or the father is assigned the disciplines in the home. Reassessing
the home components structure; would be in the order:

Elohim —The initiator
Man - Provider and disciplinarian
Woman - the Home maker
The church provides counseling and moral support.

Chapter Five

Elohiym - The Initiator

All things begin with Yeshua (Jesus), the author and the finisher of our faith, (Hebrews 12:2)

Romans 11:36King James Version (KJV) *36 For of him, and through him, and to him, are all things: to whom be glory for ever. Amen*

God is clearly the initiator of all things. He spoke all things into existence including the spirit and the soul of man. But the body, he formed with His hands.

He spoke the spirit into existence.

Genesis 1:26King James Version (KJV)
26 And God said, Let us make man in our image, after our likeness: and let them have dominion over the fish of the sea, and over the fowl of the air, and over the cattle, and over all the earth, and over every creeping thing that creepeth upon the earth.
(Detail: Chapter Seven - The Home Maker)

He spoke the soul into existence. **Genesis 1:27King James Version (KJV)**
27 So God created man in his own image, in the image of God created he him; male and female created he them
(Detail: Chapter Seven - The Home Maker)

He formed man with his hand. **Genesis 2:7King James Version (KJV)**
7 And the Lord God formed man of the dust of the ground, and breathed into his nostrils the breath of life; and man became a living soul.
(Detail: Chapter Seven - The Home Maker)

The importance of Family to God is already mentioned in chapter two by the first letter of the first word in the Hebrew bible. He wanted man (אדם ʾādam) to be happy. When man (אדם ʾadam) was showing signs of loneliness, God did not say he was going to make the man a wife, but he stipulated the duty of the wife as; "a help meet."

Genesis 2:18King James Version (KJV) *18 And the Lord God said, It is not good that the man should be alone; I will make him an help (עזר ʿēzer) meet (נגד neged) for him.*

Opposite not Opposition

נגד neged means to be opposite and toward; woman is directly in front of man, but looking back facing him, opposite not in opposition. God's given right for women is to be opposite, but the "pattern" of the world through "women's right" promotes opposition, in the hope of equality. I beg to differ; because in their effort to elevate women's status, they are unconsciously admitting that woman is in a lower level requiring elevation. I suggest that for someone to be standing opposite another person; they are equal in elevation, or standing on the same level.

In their narrative, the women's right movements are admitting that women are weak and needed help. Speaking of help, that is what women are designed to do.

עזר ʿezer means aid or help. The question is, who needs help? In the context of Genesis 2:18; one can deduce that man needs help. The Hebrew word עזרʿezer comes from the Hebrew root word עזר ʿāzar, meaning to surround, to encircle.

The rib God used to build the woman.

Woman was first mentioned in Genesis 2:22, the Hebrew word אשה ishshah means woman, wife, sometime used as female.

The origin of the word can be found in Genesis 2:23 where Adam said "She shall be called Woman because she was taken out of Man."

אשה ishshah *To bear children* Genesis 18:11King James Version (KJV)

11 Now Abraham and Sarah were old and well stricken in age; and it ceased to be with Sarah after the **manner of women**.

Genesis 2:23King James Version (KJV) *23 And Adam said, This is now bone of my bones, and flesh of my flesh: she shall be called Woman,* (אשה ishshah) *because she was taken out of Man.* (איש ʾiysh)

For the first time we see the introduction of the Hebrew word איש ʾiysh translated man or an individual. Sometimes used for male and husband.

Raising a family.

Too much emphasis is put on materialistic gifts we give to our children to gain their trust, but we neglect the emotion and spiritual impartation.

These come through the words we speak to them even as infants, a subject to be covered in details in our discussions of Marriage counseling suggestions; chapter eleven.

First we ascertain the reason Elohiym wants a man and a woman to have children and raise a family.

Record of the first birth.

Genesis 4:1King James Version (KJV)

And Adam knew Eve his wife; and she conceived, <u>and bare</u> (תלד tēled)
Cain, and said, I have gotten a man from the Lord

תלד tēled is the inflection of the Hebrew root word ילד yalad which means to bear child, to bring forth and bring up children, be delivered, declare pedigrees. Because ילד yalad is the root or Qal stem, it is articulated in 3msg (third person masculine singular PAST TENSE) "he declared pedigree."

Interesting to note that תלד tēled is the "yiqtol form" of ילד yalad with the Hebrew letter "ת" changing the tense and gender to continuous and feminine respectively. Thus should read, "she is giving birth."

While the man declares pedigree (the recorded ancestry or lineage of a person or family), the woman is always going to be the one that bears the child.

In our effort to answer the question why Elohim encourages man and woman to have children we look at another Hebrew word relative to ילד yalad

ילד yeled meaning offspring, lad and also mean **fruit**. Reminds us of God issuing the first ever instruction to Adam (the human).

Genesis 1:28King James Version (KJV)

28 And God blessed them, and God said unto them, Be fruitful, and
multiply, ….

Chapter Six

Man - The Provider and Disciplinarian

Psalm 145 amazingly layout for us what is expected of a male. Together with Proverbs 31; and few more; they are known as "acrostics" using the sequence of Hebrew alphabets as first letter of the first word of each verse.

The duty of the father cannot be underestimated; as we will see in a latter chapter, but suffice to mention; he is responsible for the spiritual up-bringing of the household, and the discipline of children.

Man has three main tasks that heads the list of his priority:

a. **Please God (fulfilling the will of God)**
b. **Provide for his family. (eat from the sweat of his brow).**
c. **Institute and establish a sincere and faith-filled atmosphere in the home, to facilitate moral and spiritual provision.**

א. #1. Aleph
HE SETS HIGH STANDARDS IN WHAT HE DOES

Psalm 145:1 King James Version (KJV) *145 I will extol thee,* (ארוממיך *'ărômimka*) *my God, O king; and I will bless thy name for ever and ever*

ארוממיך arômimka means I shall exalt or praise you. It is certain, the man is a worshipper, I suggest that he should be teaching and leading the household in the same manner. Interestingly the letter א is prefixed to the Hebrew word רומם *rûmām* changing the tense of the word to "continuous tense." Worship and praise should be a continuous event in the home. The man/husband is one that exalts God and blesses His name forever. The husband made a long term commitment; to bless and exalt Adonay "forever and ever." More importantly, he sets high standards for himself always. The example he set before his family. When man is based and founded on the Word of God; he will recognize the role of the woman.

<h2 style="text-align:center">ב # 2 bet
HE IS COMITTED DAILY</h2>

Psalm 145:2King James Version (KJV) *2 Every day* (בכל-יום b^ekāl-yôm) *will I bless thee; and I will praise thy name for ever and ever.*

בכל-יום b^ekāl-yôm Two words are joined together, and it means "in all the day." He confirms his desire to be a worshipper everyday. The Hebrew word כל meaning "all," is prefixed with the Hebrew letter ב bet providing the preposition "in." translated as "in all" or "Every."

In verse one, the husband committed long term, in verse two; he made short term promise; day by day.

Consistency will register into the minds of children; when one worships everyday; the images, the sound, the memory of that will stay with your children.

<h2 style="text-align:center">ג # 3 gimel
HE KNOWS THE GOD HE SERVES</h2>

Psalm 145:3King James Version (KJV) *3 Great* (גדול gadowl) *is the Lord, and greatly to be praised; and his greatness is unsearchable.*

This Hebrew word generally means large or great. Comes from the root word גלל **galal** meaning to make large, to exceed, also means to boast. One should boast about his/her God.

The man knows that God is immeasurable, and inexhaustible.

Psalm 44:8King James Version (KJV) *8 In God we boast all the day long, and praise thy name for ever. Selah.*

ד # 4 daleth
HE ENSURES GENERATIONS AFTER HIM WILL FEAR GOD, AND DE-CLARE GOD'S GREAT WORK

Psalm 145:4King James Version (KJV) *4 One generation (דור dôwr) shall praise thy works to another, and shall declare thy mighty acts.*

The word means generation, the time from one's birth, to the birth of one's first child. Ironically, the Hebrew word for "male" is; זכר zākār, meaning to remember, to mark (to be recognized). Every child is marked and recognized by the father's DNA as scientifically proven.

The husband has the responsibility to ensure the continuance of the family generation, declaring the mighty acts of God; i.e. blessings for the generations after him.

Speaking male and generation; the Hebrew word for boy or a young man is; ילד yeled - boy, young man. It comes from the root word; ילד **yālād** meaning to bear young, bring forth children. The same root derives the word ילדה **yaldah** meaning a lass, young girl.

ה he
HIS MIND PERCIEVES POSITIVE AND GREATNESS

Psalm 145:5King James Version (KJV) *5 I will speak of the glorious (הדר hăḏar) honour of thy majesty, and of thy wondrous works.*

הדר haďar means honor. Gauging from the vast and countless honor and majesty of God that are all positive, one can deduce that man's narrative is filled with countless positive thoughts, words, and works.

Though translated as "speak," the Hebrew word **is שׂוח** suwach meaning to meditate, muse pensively. The man's deepest thoughts are all about positive and greatness through Messiah.

ו wav
HE FEARS THE LORD

Psalm 145:6King James Version (KJV) *6 And men shall speak of the might (ועזוז veʿezuwz) of thy terrible acts: and I will declare thy greatness*

ועזוז veʿezûwz means strength. Fear of the Lord is not sign of weakness; it is strength. The central word prefixed with ו wav, thus the conjunction "and," is עזוז ʿāzûz meaning forcible, power, strong, correctly translated as "might.

The man is also aware of what it is to fear the Lord;

Deuteronomy 6:2King James Version (KJV) *2 That thou mightest fear the Lord thy God, to keep all his statutes and his command-meets, which I command thee, thou, and thy son, and thy son's son, all the days of thy life; and that thy days may be prolonged.*

ז zayin
HE SPEAKS THE GOODNESS OF GOD TO HIMSELF

Psalm 145:7King James Version (KJV) *7 They shall abundantly utter the memory (זכר zeker) of thy great goodness, and shall sing of thy righteousness*

זכר zeker is translated "memory," from the root word זכר zākār to remember. Specific mention of the abundance in the goodness of God. Abundance is translated from the Hebrew word רב rab_meaning increase that is limitless, continues to grow as long as one proclaims the goodness and sings of His righteousness. Worth noticing the word "utter," which could be perceived as to speak or say, because it comes from the Hebrew word נבע nābaʿ, meaning to gush forth, to flow in abundance in an almost uncontrollable manner; further conjugated in this verse as "yiqtol" in the "hiphil" verbal stem. thus the word; יביעו yabîʿû with the suffix ו supplying the subject as 3rd person plural giving us the phrase: "they shall abundantly utter."

The study of Hebrew verbs turns up this peculiar stem called "hiphil." it means that the verb is reflexive – the subject per-forms the action on himself/herself. this verse specifically telling us that the man speak good things to himself always.

ח chet
HE FINDS SOLACE IN THE GRACE OF GOD

Psalm 145:8King James Version (KJV) 8 *The Lord is gracious,* (חנון chanuwn) *and full of compassion; slow to anger, and of great mercy.*

חנון chanuwn translated as "gracious" from the root word;

חנן chanan meaning to stoop in kindness to an inferior. to find favor. The man learns to be gracious and compassionate by observing the Word of God. the only way he can be gracious and compassionate toward others, is if learns to be gracious and compassionate to himself.

ט tet
HE APPRECIATES THE WORKS OF GOD

Psalm 145:9King James Version (KJV) *9 The Lord is good* (טוב towb) *to all: and his tender mercies are over all his works.*

טוב tôwb Re assurance that all man is good because we are God's workmanship.

Ephesians 2:10King James Version (KJV) *10 For we are his workmanship, created in Christ Jesus unto good works, which God hath before ordained that we should walk in them*

TThe man is confident and content with what God has created him to be.

י yod
HE IS A WORSHIPER

Psalm 145:10King James Version (KJV) *10 All thy works shall* praise

(יודך yowdoka)*thee, O Lord; and thy saints shall bless thee .*יודך yôwdôka The central word is ידה yādah meaning to stretch out (the hand), praise, worship, acknowledge. in this verse however, the word is inflected with the yiqtol to give us יודך yôwdôka suggesting a continuation of the same throughout generations.

All thy works is summarized in the following:

Deuteronomy 10:14King James Version (KJV) *14 Behold, the heav-en and the heaven of heavens is the Lord's thy God, the earth also, with all that therein is.*

Included are the saints; who are expected to kneel before God. The word "bless" is translated from the Hebrew word ברך bārak, meaning to kneel.

כ kaph
UNDERSTANDS THE POWER AND THE GLORY OF GOD

Psalm 145:11King James Version (KJV) *11 They shall speak of* the glory (כבוד kᵉbowd) *of thy kingdom, and talk of thy power;* כבוד kᵉbôwd – the word means glory. this verse still refers to all the works of God as summarized in Deut. 10:14; but in addition to praise and blessing; they also need to talk and speak about the power and the glory of Adonay.

The kingdom of God dominated by three things; that those belong should observe.

Righteousness Peace Joy (strength) of the Holy Ghost **Romans 14:17King James Version (KJV)**

17 For the kingdom of God is not meat and drink; but righteous-ness, and peace, and joy in the Holy Ghost.

Power mentioned is גדול gadowl meaning, large, mighty, huge and great. the mere sight of his power is intimidating.

In Yeshua the man knows that power has been given to him to fight the enemy.

Luke 10:19King James Version (KJV)
19 Behold, I give unto you power to tread on serpents and scorpions, and over all the power of the enemy: and nothing shall by any means hurt you.

ל lamed
HE CHOOSES TO BE A STUDENT AND TEACHER OF THE WORD

Psalm 145:12King James Version (KJV) *12 **To make known** (להריע lᵉhûdîᶜa) **to the** sons of men his mighty acts, and the glorious majesty of his kingdom*

להריע lᵉhûdîᶜa This word is a conjugation of the Hebrew word

"ידע yādaᶜ" meaning to know. The word is inflected in the "Hiphil Stem," giving a causative context. He causes other people to know, and he cause or drive himself to learn.

Luke 11:28King James Version (KJV)
28 But he said, Yea rather, blessed are they that hear the word of God, and keep it

מ mayim
HE YEARNS FOR GOD TO HAVE DOMINION
OF HIS GENERA-TIONS AFTER HIM

Psalm 145:13King James Version (KJV) *13 Thy kingdom* (מלכותך malkûtᵉkā) *is an everlasting kingdom, and thy dominion en-dureth throughout all generations.*

מלכותך malkûtᵉkā - meaning your kingdom. The man acknowledges that God's kingdom is an everlasting kingdom. The word "dominion" comes from the Hebrew root word, משל māshal. Man adheres to the Lord's rulership. Further qualifies the Kingdom as one that endures forever.

Because the Kingdom endures forever, giving hope to man, that the generations that follows are blessed because of his obedience and reverence of the Kingdom of God. He recognizes that serving is not only beneficial to him, but to the generations that follow.

Acts 16:31King James Version (KJV)
31 And they said, Believe on the Lord Jesus Christ, and thou shalt be saved, and thy house.

Luke 11:28King James Version (KJV)
28 But he said, Yea rather, blessed are they that hear the word of God, and keep it

נ nun
HE HAS A POSITIVE ATTITUDE

Does not dwell on the negative

NOTE: Psalm 145 provides no verse to the letter נ nun, for unspecified reason. But one speculates using verses thirteen and fourteen.

Verse thirteen speaks of the Kingdom of God that endures forever. Verse fourteen presents an interesting twist stating that God upholds the fallen.

The word fall come from the Hebrew word נפלים neᵖhalîym. The root is נפל nāphāl, meaning to fall.

The same word was used in Genesis 6:4 describing the giants.

Genesis 6:4King James Version (KJV) *4 There were giants in the earth in those days; and also after that, when the sons of God came in unto the daughters of men, and they bare children to them, the same became mighty men which were of old, men of renown.*

He does not dwell on the past, regarding his fallen state.

Philippians 3:13King James Version (KJV)
13 Brethren, I count not myself to have apprehended: but this one thing I do, forgetting those things which are behind, and reaching forth unto those things which are before

ס samek

HE COMFORTS AND ENCOURAGES
PEOPLE WHEN THEY STRUG-GLE

Psalm 145:14King James Version (KJV) 4 **The** Lord upholdeth (סומך somek) all that fall, and raiseth up all those that be bowed down.

סומך sômēk This word comes from the root word; סמך sāmāk meaning to prop up, to take hold of. Interesting to note that the objects of upholding are those who fall. The word fall come from the Hebrew **word נפלים neᵖhalîym.** The root is נפל N45aphāl

Man knows that the Lord upholds everyone in their fallen state. But one needs to bow down; to be raised up. Raised up is the translation of the Hebrew word זקף zāqāp meaning to raise or comfort.

He encourages people to endure, and having faith in God.

2 Corinthians 1:4King James Version (KJV) *4 Who comforteth us in all our tribulation, that we may be able to comfort them which are in any trouble, by the comfort wherewith we ourselves are comforted of God.*

ע ayin
HE IS PATIENT

Psalm 145:15King James Version (KJV) 15 **The eyes (עיני** eyney) **of all wait** upon thee; and thou givest them their meat in due season עֵינֵי ʿēynēy This word comes from the word עֵינֵי ʿayin; His eyes are always fixed on the author and finisher of faith: Yeshua Mashiach. Circumstances does not move him, he is patient.

Hebrews 12:2King James Version (KJV)
2 Looking unto Jesus the author and finisher of our faith; who for the joy that was set before him endured the cross, despising the shame, and is set down at the right hand of the throne of God.

פ peh
HE IS SATISFIED OF WHO HE IS

Psalm 145:16King James Version (KJV) *16 Thou openest* (פותח putheach) ***thine*** *hand, and satisfiest the desire of every living thing.*

פותח pûtheach, is a derivative of the word פתח pātach meaning to open, to be loose, to let go free. The insertion of the letter "wav," "ו changes the verb into a present participle used as the adjective "opening" hand. The hand of God that is opening and flowing with uniquely designed provision for every uniquely designed individual. The man is satisfied that he and every individual is special in the sight of God.

Hebrews 13:5King James Version (KJV) *5 Let your conversation be without covetousness; and be content with such things as ye have: for he hath said, I will never leave thee, nor forsake thee.*

צ tsadi
HE IS A SERVANT TO RIGHTEOUSNESS

Psalm 145:17King James Version (KJV) *17 **The** Lord is righteous* (צדיק tsadiq) *in all his ways, and holy in all his works*

צדיק tsadîq Means righteous. The man understands that he is uniquely designed by a Holy God who is righteous in ALL his ways; he has an obligation to be always a servant to righteousness.

Romans 6:18King James Version (KJV) *18 Being then made free from sin, ye became the servants of righteousness.*

In every situations, he will always choose to be on the side of righteousness.

ק qoph
HIS TRUST IS IN GOD

Psalm 145:18King James Version (KJV) *18 **The** Lord is nigh* (קרוב qarob) *unto all them that call upon him, to all that call upon him in truth*

קרוב qārôb means to be near. The man knows he can trust someone who is always near. **Hebrews 13:5King James Version (KJV)** *5 Let your conversation be without covetousness; and be content with such things as ye have: for he hath said, I will never leave thee, nor forsake thee.*

ר resh
HE UNDERSTANDS THE WILL OF GOD

Psalm 145:19King James Version (KJV) *19 **He will fulfil** (רצון ratson) **the** desire of them that fear him: he also will hear their cry, and will save them.*

רצון ratsôn means pleasure, delight, desire, will, favour. This verse can be confusing because two words: "will" and "desire" are associated with the word רצון ratsôn. The same word used in the book of Mathew, when Yeshua spoke of his Father's WILL.

Matthew 7:21King James Version (KJV) *21 Not every one that saith unto me, Lord, Lord, shall enter into the kingdom of heaven; but he that doeth the will (רצון ratsôn) of my Father which is in heaven.*

The man knows how to please God, because that is the will of his Heavenly Father, to please Him.

שׁ shin
HE GUARDS HIS HEART

Psalm 145:20King James Version (KJV) *20* **The** *Lord preserveth*(שׁומר shomer) *all them that love him: but all the wicked will he destroy*

שׁומר shômēr is a present participle which translated, "guarding" of God. A derivative of the Hebrew word רמשׁ shāmar meaning to keep, to guard. The same word was used in Numbers chapter six for "benediction."

Numbers 6:24King James Version (KJV) *The Lord bless thee, and keep* (שׁומר shāmar) *thee*

The Lord keeps him and guards him; his duty is to guard his own heart; that is his responsibility.

Notice the different translation used by KJV and NIV of the Hebrew word רמושׁshômēr.

Proverbs 4:23King James Version (KJV)
23 <u>*Keep*</u> (שׁומר shāmar) *thy heart with all diligence; for out of it are the issues of life.*

Proverbs 4:23New International Version (NIV) *23 Above all else, <u>guard</u>* (שׁומר shāmar) *your heart, for everything you do flows from it*

ת taw

HIS MOUTH SPEAKS THE ABUNDANCE OF HIS HEART

Psalm 145:21King James Version (KJV) 21 My mouth shall speak the praise (**תהלת** tᵉhilath) of the Lord: and let all flesh bless his holy name for ever and ever **תהלת** tᵉhilath

The man is overwhelmed with his maker, his creator and now his Heavenly Father; as the spirit of God reveals to him. His body his soul and his spirit saturated with life for God, that he speaks nothing but the glory and praises of God.

Luke 6:45King James Version (KJV)
45 A good man out of the good treasure of his heart bringeth forth that which is good; and an evil man out of the evil treasure of his heart bringeth forth that which is evil: for of the abundance of the heart his mouth speaketh.

Chapter Seven

The Home Maker

The verses we use represent the qualities of a "home maker." first the moral instructions; chastity, justice, mercy and temperance, what follows is teaching by example.

This proverb was for king Lemuel, a prophesy by his mother. There is no other mention of this king in the scriptures except the two places in Proverbs chapter thirty one. Some say it is a symbolic name for king Solomon, speaking the prophesy of Bathsheba his mother.

The child does not belong to her.

Proverbs 31:1King James Version (KJV) *The words of king Lemuel, the prophecy that his mother taught him.*

What can we deduce from this verse? A mother knows exactly; where the son comes from. The name Lᵉmuel comes from two Hebrew word:

למו *lamuw* is a separable prefix preposition meaning from or belonging to אל *el* means God. Lᵉmuel means "belonging to God.

If you were a parent; who would you give your children to, if they do not belong to you? Hannah knew that her son Samuel belong to God. After she gave birth to her son, she took her back to where he belongs.

1 Samuel 1:22King James Version (KJV) *22 But Hannah went not up; for she said unto her husband, I will not go up until the child be weaned, and then I will bring him, that he may appear before the Lord, and there abide for ever.*

For whatever reason the king's name becomes Lemuel, the intention is clear, telling us that our children do not belong to us; they come from God and they are going back to God. A home maker knows the value of all included in the household. She treats the children with respect.

Where do we come from?

The obvious answer would be mother and father. The scripture reveals to us something I hope you find interesting.

Jeremiah 1:5King James Version (KJV) *5 Before I formed thee in the belly I knew thee; and before thou camest forth out of the womb I sanctified thee, and I ordained thee a prophet unto the nations.*

One can deduce from Jeremiah 1:5 that God knew us before we were formed in our mother's womb. God however, acknowledges the part our parents play, that he listed the requirements for children to honour mother and father for the child to inherit long life in the Ten Commandments.

Exodus 20:12King James Version (KJV)
12 Honour thy father and thy mother: that thy days may be long upon the land which the Lord thy God giveth thee.

From a natural perspective, it is hard to understand, how God knows us before conception, which suggest that we exist in another form other than the body before we were formed in the belly.

Let us look into some verses in the scriptures. Suffice to mention that the complete man is divided in three, Spirit, Soul and Body in the order they were created. The body is the last to be formed.

<u>SPIRIT</u> (the spirit was established)

The Hebrew word for spirit is רוח **ruach** meaning wind, spirit.

When we speak of the Spirit of God, we speak of the "wind of God." I am reminded of Peter in Mathew 14:30, while he walked toward Jesus on the water, the bible says; "*But when he saw the **wind** boisterous, he was afraid.*" Peter was aware of the wind before he left the boat; I suggest he may have seen spirits and was afraid.

<u>Genesis 1:26</u>King James Version (KJV)
26 And God said, Let us make (עשה asah) man in our image, after our likeness: and let them have dominion over the fish of the sea, and over the fowl of the air, and over the cattle, and over all the earth, and over every creeping thing that creepeth upon the earth.

-עשה *asah* - means to appoint, call forth, describe the process of construction, to complete. If God knew us before we were formed in our mother's womb and as suggested earlier, we exist in another form other than the body, could this be where our spirit, is known by God?

<u>SOUL</u> (the soul was created)

Soul is translated from the Hebrew word נפש nephesh, meaning breath, the inner being with its thoughts and emotions, (Judges 10:16)

<u>Genesis 1:27</u>King James Version (KJV)
27 So God created (ברא bārāʾ) man in his own image, in the image of God created he him; male and female created he them.

ברא **bārāʾ**- means to select, to choose, to feed. Sometimes used to clear timber (Joshua 17:15) or to make fat (1 Samuel 2:29) Note the meaning of the word ברא bāraʾ– select, choose, feed, these are administered in our minds and understanding. I suggest that soul is where we reason, make decisions and select. **<u>BODY</u> (the body was formed)**

Body was translated from the Hebrew word בשר basar meaning flesh, body.

Genesis 2:7King James Version (KJV) *7 And the Lord God formed (יצר- yatsar) man of the dust of the ground, and breathed into his nostrils the breath of life; and man became a living soul.*

יצר- yatsar - means to squeeze into shape, to mould into a form, especially as a porter.

Merging Of The Three

Now we look at the scripture where God merged the spirit, soul and the body.

<u>**Genesis 2:7**</u>**King James Version (KJV)**
7 And the Lord God formed man of the dust of the ground, and breathed into his nostrils (אפים ʾāphiym) the breath of life (חיים נשמת nishmoth hayiym); and man became a living soul (נפש חיה nephesh hayah).

We will extract some words and phrase from this verse to give a clear picture of what God did to merge the spirit, soul, and body. נשמת חיים **nishmath chayiym** should have been translated as *breaths of lives*: because they are in plural form. One can deduce that every human on earth is created and have living souls then. Scriptural proof that **nishmath** is the spirit of man.

Proverbs 20:27King James Version (KJV)
27 The spirit (נשמת nishmath) of man is the candle of the Lord, searching all the inward parts of the belly.

⁷ אפים **aphiym** means noses in plural form. God was breathing into many noses.

נפש היה **nephesh hayah** means living soul. This separates human from animals. Human has a living soul. The Hebrew for animal comes from two Hebrew words: בה beh meaning "in." the other is מה mah meaning "what is." Therefore in a בהמה behmah or animals; in it, is what it is. Animals cannot be anything other than what it is already.

Human are living souls, they can grow up to something better. Have the ability to excel in whatever they do.

SUMMARY

Step 1 – God formed the body from the dust (Genesis 2:7)

Step 2 – he then breathed into the nostril the spirit and soul spoken in Genesis 1:26 and Genesis 1:27 respectively.

Step 3 – when we die, the process is reversed; the spirit and soul leave the body, to go back where it came from. Likewise, the body returns to the dust, where it came from.

Moral Instruction The Home maker is aware that children are individuals known by God. Some say that children are gifts from Elohiym to the parents. A scripture comes to mind, Paslm 127:3.

Psalm 127:3Amplified Bible, Classic Edition (AMPC)
3 Behold, children are a heritage (נחל nachal) from the Lord, the fruit of the womb a reward.

נחל nachal is not quite the "gift" as suggested, otherwise it would have the Hebrew word מתן matthan a derivative of the Hebrew root word נתן Nathan meaning to give.

נחל nachal means to receive or take property as a permanent possession. However in both cases children are given to us.

Chapter Eight

The Nursing Process

My Son, Son of My Womb, Son of my Vow

Proverbs 31:2King James Version (KJV)*2 What, my son? and what, the son of my womb? and what, the son of my vows?*

Further to her recognition of the uniqueness her children represent, she gave three different insights; or an accurate and deep understanding of what a child represents.

My Son - the word used here, is בַּר bar, Aramaic equivalent of בֵּן ben, Hebrew for "son." the builder of the family name. From the very early stage of the child; the mother attend to majority of the nursing. She feeds the child hope.

Psalm 22:9King James Version (KJV)
9 *But thou art he that took me out of the womb: thou didst make me hope when I was upon my mother's breasts*

She believes in the child and faith that he is going to fulfil the call of God in his life. Speaking of faith, ironically it is translated from the Hebrew root word; אָמַן 'āman. Another usage of this Hebrew word is nurse and nurture.

Nurture and Nourishment, and Nurse

Ruth 4:16King James Version (KJV)
16 And Naomi took the child, and laid it in her bosom, and became nurse (אָמַן ʾāman) ***unto it.***

The Raising Children Network says the following *about early child development.*

"Development is the term used to describe the changes in your child's physical growth, as well as her ability to learn the social, emotional, behavior, thinking and communication skills she needs for life. All of these areas are linked, and each depends on and influences the others.

In the first five years of life, **your child's brain develops more and faster** than at any other time in his life.

The early experiences your child has the things;

- he sees
- hears
- touches
- smells and
- tastes stimulate his brain, creating millions of connections. This is when foundations for learning, health and behavior throughout life are laid down."

The home maker knows fully well the importance of this early years of the child, while the man is away to provide for his family, she spends time as part of her duty to teach the children about life and living.

Son of my womb - Also used as children in general, evident in the following verse.

Genesis 3:16King James Version (KJV) ***16 Unto the woman he said, I will greatly multiply thy sorrow and thy conception; in sorrow*** *thou shalt bring forth children; (בנים bānîym) and thy desire shall be to thy husband, and he shall rule over thee.* The womb has a special significance. Translated from the Hebrew word; בטן beten. The meaning is womb. Apart from its obvious usage as the nutritional headquarters for the child in uteri, the home maker recognizes that this is also the place where God calls his elect.

Jeremiah 1:5King James Version (KJV)*5 Before I formed thee in the belly I knew thee; and before thou camest forth out of the womb I sanctified thee, and I ordained thee a prophet unto the nations.*

Son of my vow

The home maker reveals the importance of a vow. Translated from the Hebrew word נדר nādār meaning vow. When making a vow, the soul is also involved, thus the close and sometimes almost telepathic connection between the mother and the child.

Numbers 30:6King James Version (KJV)
6 And if she had at all an husband, when she vowed, or uttered ought out of her lips, wherewith she bound her soul;

Raising of the king

The Hebrew word מלך **melek**, translated as king is usually associated with a kingdom where he reigns. In many biblical contexts, the term is simply a general term, denoting an individual with power and authority.

I believe individuals have the right to exert their God-given power and authority in their own unique little kingdom, without offending others. Make their own choices, and face consequences like Adam and Eve at the garden.

I suggest we are kings and queens in own right, so as the child leaves behind the formative years moving toward puberty and adulthood, with the increased hormonal behavior, the home maker begins the warning of sexual immorality.

Proverbs 31:3-4King James Version (KJV)
3 Give not thy strength unto women, nor thy ways to that which destroyeth kings. 4 It is not for kings, O Lemuel, it is not for kings to drink wine; nor for princes strong drink:

In case you have not heard, I want to let you into a little secret.

The King James Translation listed the names of kings and the number of year they reign twenty nine times. For clarity in identification, the mother's names are mentioned, unlike some cultures where the father's name is mentioned together with the child.

1 Kings 6 times 2 Kings 13 times
2 Chronicles 9 times Jeremiah once.

Twenty nine times the bible mentioned the mothers name. even when things do not turn out as expected; the report will always include the mother's name.

Leviticus 24:11King James Version (KJV)
*11 And the Israelitish woman's son blasphemed the name of the Lord, and cursed. And they brought him unto Moses: (**and his mother's name was Shelomith,** the daughter of Dibri, of the tribe of Dan:)*

May I suggest that the mother, (the home maker) is responsible for the implication of upbringing according to the word of Elohim, taught to the family by the disciplinarian, the father.

Give not thy strength:

The word strength is translated from the Hebrew word חיל chayil. This word has the basic idea of strength and influence. Also of wealth and war. God is often seen as the supplier of this strength.

2 Samuel 22:35King James Version (KJV)
35 He teacheth my hands to war (חיל chayil); so that a bow of steel is broken by mine arms.

Habakkuk 3:19King James Version (KJV)
19 The Lord God is my strength, (חיל hayil) and he will make my feet like hinds' feet, and he will make me to walk upon mine high places. To the chief singer on my stringed instruments.

Why is he not warned against lying or stealing, but of sexual immorality, and woman?

One is reminded of Numbers chapter thirty verse six, when the female through maternal connection is bound by the soul to the son because he is the son of her vow.

She is warning the king that, not only is he going to have soul-tie to the woman through sexual connection, his strength, given by Elohim will be annulled because Elohiym cannot work with sin. Thus the destruction of the kingdom. He will be tied emotionally to the woman.

One only has to look at the example of Samson's demise.

A Drink Or Two

The next two verses are for those that believe, they belong to God.

Proverbs 31:4King James Version (KJV) *4 It is not for kings, O Lemuel, it is not for kings to drink wine; nor for princes strong drink:*

Notice how she reminded him by saying for the second and the last time: "O Lemuel," meaning do not forget you belong to God.

To help bring clarity to what I believe, an area that continues to grow greyer; we summon two scriptures.

Some born again believers are claiming that one glass of drink is not harmful. I am not here to say if they are right or wrong. I am simply going to share the word as Paul commanded Timothy, rightly dividing the word of truth.

2 Timothy 2:15King James Version (KJV)*15 Study to shew thyself approved unto God, a workman that needeth not to be ashamed, rightly dividing the word of truth.*

Genesis 27:28King James Version (KJV)
28 Therefore God give thee of the dew of heaven, and the fatness of the earth, and plenty of corn and wine (תירוש tirowsh)

תירוש *tirowsh* meaning fresh grape juice, not fermented.

Proverbs 31:4King James Version (KJV)
4 It is not for kings, O Lemuel, it is not for kings to drink wine;(יין *yayin*) nor for princes strong drink:

יין *yayin* meaning fermented wine, intoxication.

Proverbs 23:31King James Version (KJV)
31 Look not thou upon the wine (יין yayin) when it is red, when it giveth his colour in the cup, when it moveth itself aright.

Why does the scripture warn about wine?

Proverbs 23:33King James Version (KJV)
33 Thine eyes shall behold strange women, (זרות zārôth) and thine heart shall utter perverse things.

The scripture alluded to a connection between wine and women, suggesting that the consumption of intoxicating drink also generate perversity.

זרות zārôth is feminine plural of the Hebrew root word זור zuwr, meaning to turn aside, and also used in the following scriptures as to "commit adultery."

Proverbs 2:16King James Version (KJV) *16 To deliver thee from the strange woman, even from the stranger which flattereth* (**החליקה. hechelîqāh**) *with her words*

החליקה hechelîqāh is a conjugation of the Hebrew root word חלק chalaq meaning "he flattered," is inflected in the "hiphil" verbal stem: החליק hecheliq suggesting a causative voice, "he was flattered," finally the suffix ה changes the subject as feminine: the strange woman will influence the king to have a double heart as well as flattering lips.

Psalm 12:2King James Version (KJV)
2 They speak vanity every one with his neighbour: with flattering (חלק chalaq) *lips and with a double heart do they speak.*

Double heart is when you say something that is not consistent with what is in your heart.

Chapter Nine

Recognizing Uniqueness

When we closed chapter five, we alluded to the notion that; The Home maker is aware that children are individuals; known by God.

Growing up in a traditional Fijian family; sons show respect of the father by "only speaking when spoken to." Things have changed now due to the higher level of our exposures to other cultures. Also the awareness, that effectiveness around the home or anywhere for that matter, demands free of unsolicited conversation.

It is regarded as disrespectful in our culture, and I believe other cultures as well, to argue your case should your father question allegation leveled at you. Through out the entire prosecutorial process, you are expected to keep quiet and take the punishment. Growing up in a communal or village set up you could hear the supposedly disciplinary words, I would say abusive, that comes from next door. Each time the sound of the belt landing on the child, you could almost feel it when it's followed by the excruciating cry from deep within the poor soul.

I usually ask, why? One of the comments I often hear is; "I own you." or, "you should appreciate me working to put food on the table."

It sounds like the children have been blamed for the father working to put food on the table.

I arrived at the conclusion, our parents believe we belong to them and they own us. I am not blaming our parents, because no one told them. The assumption of parents owning children, is flawed because it is disqualified by Jeremiah chapter one verse five.

Jeremiah 1:5King James Version (KJV)5 *Before I formed thee in the belly I knew thee; and before thou camest forth out of the womb I sanctified thee, and I ordained thee a prophet unto the nations.*

I repeat: "*before I formed thee in the belly, I knew thee.*" I suggest that before the parents knew each other; God knew the children. This raises several questions;

1. Do we exist in any other form before being conceived?
2. Do we exist in spiritual form before we are formed in our mother's womb?
3. Do we exist in an emotional form?
4. Is there evidence to show that God knew all of us; including our parents, and our grand parents?

The answer is yes to all of the questions.

More about that later, right now I want to draw your attention to Proverbs chapter thirty one verse one.

I remind us again, that what I am about to share can and will only be understood if God builds the house.

Respect for the child

Proverbs 31:1King James Version (KJV) *The words of king Lemuel, the prophecy that his mother taught him.*

This HEBREW word (למואל) Lemuel is mentioned only twice in the entire

King James Version of the bible. Both in Proverbs chapter thirty one; verses 1 and 4.

A mother; in this case Bathsheba addressing his son king Solomon Lemuel.

A derivative of two Hebrew words;

1. למו lamuw – is separable prefix pronoun meaning to, or for.
2. אל 'el. Short for God, god, mighty.

The mother is acknowledging that her son is for God, her son belongs to God. If Psalms 24 is an indicator saying that the earth is the Lord's and everything in it; and those that live in it.

Children are gifts from God to the parents. I suggest we treat them the way we treat the children of a family visiting for the weekend.

Speaking at a conference I asked mothers; "when was the last time you cook the best meal for just your family? Careful the first time you do; the children will ask, mum are we having visitors?"

They notice the only time you cook such meal is when visitors come home.

The verse is testimony for the
The Virtuous Woman

Proverbs 31:10King James Version (KJV) *10 Who can find a virtuous woman? for her price is far above rubies*

The English word "virtuous" is translated from the Hebrew word; חיל transliterated *chayil.* Meaning a force. A masculine noun meaning strength, wealth, army, able, activity. A verse well known to use this word is 2 Samuel 22:40

2 Samuel 22:40King James Version (KJV) *40 For thou hast girded me with strength (חיל chayil) to battle: them that rose up against me hast thou subdued under me.*

Since we are king and queens in our own right, we need to be seen upholding the law and judgement we assert, not only to the people, also to us.

Proverbs 31:5King James Version (KJV) *5 Lest they drink, and forget the law, and pervert the judgment of any of the aflicted*

The Home Maker stresses the importance of not compromising the law by the influence of intoxicating wine. Enough said about wine

Chapter Ten

Acrostic

The next verses in Proverbs 31:10-31 we observe that the first word of each verse in the Hebrew bible starts with the Hebrew letters in their alphabetical order. A picture that tells us the manner, and the integrity with which the Home Maker conducts herself in her duties to her family. Another interesting aspect of the Hebrew language is the absence of numerical value and the usage of the letters in its place

א aleph #1

WOMAN OF ABILITY AND INFLUENCE

Proverbs 31:10King James Version (KJV)*10 Who can find a virtuous woman? for her price is far above rubies.*

First word in *The Hebrew Bible* is אשת-חיל 'ēsheth chayil Comes from the Hebrew word אשה *transliterated* 'ishāh meaning woman. Join to the Hebrew word חיל **chayil** means **strength** and **influence**. King James translated as "virtuous." Speak of those that are strong for war. **Righteous in behaviour** (1 Kings 1:52) virtuous character (Ruth 3:11)

The Home Maker is not a weak person; but strong and righteous.

ב bayit #2

WOMAN OF TRUST

Proverbs 31:11King James Version (KJV)*11 The heart of her husband doth safely trust in her, so that he shall have no need of spoil.*

First word in *The Hebrew Bible* is בטח bātach

בטח means to trust, to express a feeling of safety. Because this verb is in the perfect form, or in the "qal" stem, it is articulated in 3msg (3rd person) thus the usage of "male" as the subject. Maybe interesting to observe the word husband; I expected to see the Hebrew word איש transliterated "ʾiysh," but the Hebrew word used is; בעלה transliterated "baˤlā." Meaning Baal or possessor. To defy political correctness to the woman, she is the "property" of the husband. And he can trust her. Both these Hebrew words appear in:

Hosea 2:16King James Version (KJV)*16 And it shall be at that day, saith the Lord, that thou shalt call me **Ishi**; and shalt call me no more **Baali.***

How the man should react, will be discussed in latter chapter.

ג gimel # 3

WOMAN WHO COMPLETES THE MAN

Proverbs 31:12King James Version (KJV)*12 She will do him good and not evil all the days of her life*

First word in *The Hebrew Bible* is גמלתהו gᵉmalathhu

This is an inflection of the Hebrew word גמל *gamal*. Meaning to treat a person well. Apart from doing good, as used in this context; this word also means to recompense another, bring to completion. The woman completes the man. Two individuals coming together as one.

Matthew 19:5King James Version (KJV)5 *And said, For this cause shall a man leave father and mother, and shall cleave to his wife: and they twain shall be one flesh?*

It is the man, not the woman that leaves mother and father to cling to the wife.

Genesis 2:24King James Version (KJV)24 Therefore shall a man leave his father and his mother, and shall cleave unto his wife: and they shall be one flesh.

ד daleth # 4

WOMAN WHO DESIRES QUALITY

Proverbs 31:13King James Version (KJV)*13 She seeketh wool, and flax, and worketh willingly with her hands*

First word in *The Hebrew Bible* is דרשה dārshāh

דרש darash is the main word here meaning to inquire or make inquisition continually. When she is knitting wool, she enquires for the quality, ensuring that her family deserves only that which is good. The word "willingly" is translated from the Hebrew word חפץ *chephets* meaning to delight and having pleasure doing things for her family.

ה he # 5

SHE ADJUST TO ALL SITUATION

Proverbs 31:14King James Version (KJV)14 She is like the merchants' ships; she bringeth her food from afar.

First word in *The Hebrew Bible* is היתה haytah

היתה haytah The last letter; ה supplies the number and gender, This very same Hebrew word, was used in Genesis 1:2 describing the state of the earth; she was without form and void. In this context, *she is* like a merchant ship.

ו wav # 6
SHE IS AN EARLY RISER

Proverbs 31:15King James Version (KJV) 15 **She riseth also while it is yet night, and** giveth meat to her household, and a portion to her maidens.

First word in *The Hebrew Bible* is ותקם vatāqām

The letter ו represent "and" but substituted in the translation as "**also.**" The main word is קם *qom* meaning to "rise." Another prefix we find in this conjugation is תtells us that the word is in the 'yiqtol' form or imperfect form. The gender is 3fsg, therefore the verse should read; "and she is rising."

ז zayin # 7
SHE IS AN ECONOMIC STRATEGIST

Proverbs 31:16King James Version (KJV)16 She considereth a field, and buyeth it: with the fruit of her hands she planteth a vineyard

First word in *The Hebrew Bible* is זממה **zammah**

From the Hebrew word זמם zamam, meaning to consider; which will give the translation. "**he considered**," but with the sufix ה, the word is translated "she considered." It denotes the action of fixing thought on an object so as to acquire it.

One need not be a genius to be an economist; one ought to be able to work out what is good for the family, as long as it is in the forefront of every decision she makes; coupled with the execution of the necessary action. For example; she might want a new dress; but the school fees is due before the next pay day. If the family is important, she will make the right decision.

Time is an entity that requires a lot of consideration, and the bible says we must buy time not sell it.

Ephesians 5:16King James Version (KJV)16 Redeeming the time, because the days are evil.

ח chet # 8
SHE IS ALERT AND PREVENTATIVE

Proverbs 31:17King James Version (KJV) [17] **She** girdeth her loins with strength, and strengtheneth her arms

First word in *The Hebrew Bible* is חגרה chāgrāh

חגרה chāgrāh is the inflection of the Hebrew root word, חגר chagar means to gird or put belt around. The ה supplies the gender of the subject. Thus "she girded…" Chagar also means to restrain on every side, to be afraid (preventative), be able to put on.

ט tet # 9
WOMAN OF DISCERNMENT AND A
TRADER WITH GOOD TASTE

Proverbs 31:18King James Version (KJV)18 **She** perceives that her merchandise is good: her candle goeth not out by night.

First word in *The Hebrew Bible* טעמה tā'amah Comes from the Hebrew root word טעם ta'am means taste, discernment, and discrete. The word has several abstract meanings; it can mean mental or spiritual perception. The ה at the end of the word again indicates the gender. Without such quality, a beautiful woman is compared to a gold ring on a pig's snout.

Proverbs 11:22King James Version (KJV) 22 As a jewel of gold in a swine's snout, so is a fair woman which is without discretion (טעם ta'am)

Another word worth checking out is translated as "merchandise." The Hebrew word is סחר sachar: meaning profit, merchandise, from the root word סחר sāchar meaning to travel around specially as a pedlar; occupy, trade and trafic, any hour of the day, even at night, according to this verse "her candle does not go out." She is a true "home maker."

י yod # 10

WOMAN WHO UNDERSTANDS THE IMPORTANCE OF MAKING THINGS WORK TOGETHER.

Proverbs 31:19King James Version (KJV)19 **She** layeth her hands to the spindle, and her hands hold the distaff.

First word in *The Hebrew Bible* ידיה yadeyha

The first Hebrew word used is יד yod, speaking of hand. Note the first three letters; ידי yadey meaning "hands" plural. ה once again indicates the gender (feminine 3sgl)

This is a multilayered verse in two different levels of interpretation. The first is about spinning wool. The second expresses what motivates and drives the home maker.

The verse describes two different parts of the hands though described with the same word. The arm is laid on the spindle, and the palm of the hand is on the distaff.

Two words we focus on :

1. כשור kiyshowr (translated as "spindle") means a director, and that is what a spindle does; it directs the spun wool, from the distaff.

But if we consider the root word of which כשור kiyshowr is derived from; it enables us to see a deeper revelation. The root is; כשר kāshēr, meaning to be straight, to be right, to succeed, to prosper. She held these principles with both hands as an inspiration, the spindle that drives and directs her. The home maker understands that being righteous is going to ensure your place in eternity, but little to do with prosperity and success unless you put both hands involved in doing the work.

2. פלך pālek meaning distaff or crutch. It is what holds the yarn, she used the palm of her hands to secure the yarn as mentioned in verse nineteen. The palm of the hands secure your hard earned profit, to be directed to the spindle where they are refined.

Proverbs 31:19King James Version (KJV)19 She layeth her hands to the spindle, (כשור kiyshowr) and her hands hold the distaff. (פלך pālek)

כ kaph # 20
SHE CARES FOR THE NEEDY

Proverbs 31:20King James Version (KJV)20 She stretcheth out her hand to the poor; yea, she reacheth forth her hands to the needy

First word in *The Hebrew Bible* כפה kāphah

כפ kaph means palm of the hand. כפה Means palm of her hand. She gives to the poor and the needy.

ל lamed # 30
SHE IS STRONG WILLED AND HAS NO FEAR

Proverbs 31:21King James Version (KJV)21 She is not afraid of the snow for her household: for all her household are clothed with scarlet.

First word in *The Hebrew Bible* לא-תירא loʾ-thiyrāʾ

לֹא loʾ means no or not; joined here to another word to form one word. The word is ירא yaraʾ meaning fear, or afraid. Notice the Hebrew letter תprefixed to ירא yārāʾ this now is an yiqtol word; the translation would be; she is not fearing.

מ mayim # 40
SHE IS SELF-CONFIDENT

Proverbs 31:22King James Version (KJV)22 She maketh herself coverings of tapestry; her clothing is silk and purple

First word in *The Hebrew Bible* מרבדים marbadîym

The main word is מרבד *marbad* meaning a covering of tapestry. The addition of suffixes מרבדים marbadiym make this word a masculine plural. Thus "coverings.

Her clothing is silk, the Hebrew word used. שש shēsh : blue fine twined linen bleached white.

Purple is royalty; she knows through Elohiym, and Yeshua, she is the child of the King and creator of the universe.

נ nun # 50
ATTENTIVE TO THE FAMILY'S DAILY SCHEDULES

Proverbs 31:23King James Version (KJV)23 Her husband is known in the gates, when he sitteth among the elders of the land

First word in *The Hebrew Bible* נודע nôdāʿ

In parsing, one will find the central word is ידע yadaʿ meaning to "acknowledge." But in this verse ידע yadaʿ is changed to a *niphal* stem by the addition of נ to the front of the word. The interesting aspect of niphal, it has passive voice, so in the context of this verse; the acknowledgement the husband gets at the meeting place, is a reflexion of the work she does preparing him for such. Maybe he is always in fresh clean attire one speculates… She ensures the husband is well respected wherever he goes, presume that applies to her children too.

ס samek # 60

SHE IS ENTERPRISING AND COMPASSIONATE

Proverbs 31:24King James Version (KJV)24 She maketh fine linen, and selleth it; and delivereth girdles unto the merchant

First word in *The Hebrew Bible* סדין **sādîyn**

This word is translated as "fine linen." In this verse. סדין sādîyn means to envelope, wrapper, thus shirt that wraps around.

She make shirt and sells them. But the girdles or aprons, she gave then free. One also notice that she has compassion for those that are disadvantaged. The verse translated "merchant" from the Hebrew word כנעני Kᵉnaʕǎniy which comes from the root word; כנע kānaʕ meaning humiliated, this is also the word that derives Canaanites.

She gives free to them that are somehow humiliated; girdles to encourage them; apron to cover their shame and encourage them to make a new beginning.

ע ayin # 70

SHE IS STRONG AND BOLD

Proverbs 31:25King James Version (KJV)25 Strength and honour are her clothing; and she shall rejoice in time to come.

First word in *The Hebrew Bible* עז ʕoz

The word עז ʕoz means strength, power, mighty and boldness. עז ʕez is a word for goat. But in the context of this verse it speaks of strength etc.

פ peh # 80
SHE IS WISE AND KIND

Proverbs 31:26King James Version (KJV)26 She openeth her mouth with wisdom; and in her tongue is the law of kindness.

First word in *The Hebrew* Bible פיה piyha

פיה piyha means mouth of her, or her mouth.

She opens her mouth only if she has anything wise and kind to say. Wisdom of God unlike knowledge and understanding is not learned in school; only God gives wisdom. Wisdom of this world can be acquired through knowledge and understanding, but the wisdom she displays is the result of her relationship with Adonay Elohim.

James 1:5King James Version (KJV)5 If any of you lack wisdom, let him ask of God, that giveth to all men liberally, and upbraideth not; and it shall be given him.

The gentleness in her demeanor, is no different when she speaks to her children, her tongue is filled with kindness and mercy.

צ tsadi # 90
SHE TEACHES THE CHILDREN HOW TO BEHAVE

Proverbs 31:27King James Version (KJV)27 She looketh well to the ways of her household, and eateth not the bread of idleness

First word in *The Hebrew Bible* צופיה tsôphiyâ

The word means to be watchful. Comes from the root word, צפה tsâphâh meaning to lean forward, look into the distance. The woman is a planner, she carefully plans for the family. And ensure the children are taught how to behave and survive in the future.

הליכות haliykowth is the inflected version of the הלך hālak meaning to walk or to go. In the participle form; it forms the phrase: the goings on. She watches what goes on in the home. The word "idleness" comes from the Hebrew word; עצלות ʿatslowth meaning indolent; (*wanting to avoid activity or exertion; lazy*). She ensures they eat and use only the fruit of their labour, not the bread of idleness.

ק qoph # 100
SHE IS HUMBLE AND ATTRACTS APPRECIATION

Proverbs 31:28King James Version (KJV)28 **Her** children arise up, and call her blessed; her husband also, and he praiseth her.

First word in *The Hebrew* Bible קמו qāmû

קם appears for the second time meaning arise…here it is inflected with pronominal suffix ו vaw ; (3mpl) third person masculine plural. (They, them)…the phrase reads as; "they arise."

The Psalmist gives us a picture every family should aspire to: the children wake up and tell their mother; be blessed, or you are a blessing. This is not flattery; but genuine appreciation. The husband whom she calls her possessor, praises her.

ר resh # 200
SHE IS UNIQUE

Proverbs 31:29King James Version (KJV)29 **Many** daughters have done virtuously, but thou excellest them all.

First word in *The Hebrew* Bible רבות rabûth

This word is plural of רבו **rabûw** meaning "increase." Thus in plural translated as "many." The verse typifies the collective resolve of her children and her husband. Though there are mothers like her out there, she is simply the best of them all.

שׁ shin # 300
SHE FEARS THE LORD

Proverbs 31:30King James Version (KJV)30 Favour is deceitful, and beauty is vain: but a woman that feareth the Lord, she shall be praised.

First word in *The Hebrew* Bible שׁקר sheqer

Untruthful comes to mind. To deal falsely, or engage in deceitful activities. Favor is translated from the same Hebrew word that brings to us Grace, at first glance it seems that Grace is deceitful. The context of this in the verse is suggesting that sadly at times when trying to gain favor, some resort to deceitful means. One can consider that favor and beauty are two things expected of a woman, but the woman who fears the Lord Shall be praised.

As mentioned earlier, if God does not build the house people labour in vain. The effort of the Home Maker will only be accomplished fully, if she fears the Lord.

ת taw # 400
SHE LEAVES BEHIND A LEGACY, WORTH SHARING.

Proverbs 31:31King James Version (KJV)31 **Give** her of the fruit of her hands; and let her own works praise her in the gates

First word in *The Hebrew Bible* תנו tᵉnû

This Hebrew word is the inflection of the root word נתן Nathan meaning to give, notice נ nun, considered a weak letter disappears, and assimilates into ת taw; thus the dot in the letter taw. The vaw ו at the end supplies the 3mpl they as the pronominal suffix. The verse shows give her; but specifically the fruit of her hands, are saying; "we give her praise. In other words, her achievements are known by the fruit of her hands.

Chapter Eleven

The Marriage Counseling Suggestions

This book was inspired by the concern with the increase in domestic violence and child rape and abuse in Fiji; perpetrated by close family members. Though we may not be able to arrest the current trend; we certainly can ensure that through the Word of God; this terrible and appalling behavior can be minimized if not eradicated altogether. The first place I believe needed to be addressed is the beginning of courtship leading to marriage; then of course the most important part; raising children. Ensuring informed upbringing is put in place.

Most of the behavior stems from broken homes; physical, emotional and verbal abuses in early childhood, even in uteri. Experiments have been conducted proving that a child have some degree of learning and listening in the womb, according to study by Samuel Lopez De Victoria. (refer reference)

The material we shared regarding the husband and the wife, and their responsibility, could be used by marriage counsellors; where we stress the importance of God building the house, in order for the home to function according to the pattern of the word of God, and not according to the pattern of the world.

I sense a deep responsibility, after researching the materials above, to suggest that a two-pronged marriage counseling approach needed to be presented in the following categories:

    a.   Marriage - based on love and the word of God
    b.   Raising a child - based on love, joy, and the word of God.

Not every couple will want to have children in the early years of marriage; however it is important to go through responsibilities should they decide to do so.

Decision making is central to carrying out this important period of marriage. *For example;* in cases where both parents work, should the wife stop working to look after the children?

Raising the children is important, and therefore great care and preparation for both father and mother is vital, when deciding to have children.

Yeshua also mention the importance children play in the Kingdom.

Matthew 18:6King James Version (KJV)6 *But whoso shall offend one of these little ones which believe in me, it were better for him that a millstone were hanged about his neck, and that he were drowned in the depth of the sea.*

The following represents pointers for marriage counsellors and of course parents. These findings are purely revelations from the word of God, it's my prayer that should someone find it useful; please share it with others.

MOTHER

God equipped women as the designated Homemaker

Earlier we spoke about the strength of women as designed by the Word of God. As deduced from Proverbs 31:12; without suggesting that man is incomplete nor trying to degrade his role, the woman completes the man. Suffice to mention that man is still the head of the home and instructed by God to multiply but man is not designed physically to give birth; thus the completion woman brings to the fulfillment of multiplying.

I applaud the women that singlehandedly provide and care for the children when the man leaves the home for whatever reason. They have the emotional fortitude and commitment to bring only the best she can for her children.

The role of the Homemaker can not be emphasized enough. The child will carry the love, attention and care for the rest of his/her life according to what they hear the father say, and to what they observe the mother does.

Proverbs 4:1King James Version (KJV) *Hear, ye children, the instruction of a father, and attend to know understanding.*

Raising children is not work but an attitude.

Mothers must know that raising a child is not just getting up in weird hours to heat the bottle; or preparing lunch for the first day at school. A responsibility designed and entrusted to mothers by the Initiator The Lord God Almighty our creator.

The home maker is responsible as early as conception.

Psalm 58:3King James Version (KJV)3 *The wicked are estranged from the womb: they go astray as soon as they be born, speaking lies.*

What you say during pregnancy is important; for the fetus can hear whilst still in the womb. According to Health line (reference)

Nurse, and instill truth and faith

Ruth 4:16King James Version (KJV)*16 And Naomi took the child, and laid it in her bosom, and became nurse (אמון 'āmown) unto it.*

Note: the word nurse brings a rather shallow understanding of what Naomi's task entails.

The word אמון 'āmown meaning training, skills. Nursing is not just feeding, bathing and changing diapers, it is about teaching life skills to a child; and they learn; not from what they hear, but what they see the mother does. It is hard for the children to understand why the mother is telling them to do something she does not.

When the mother neglects her work at home she is not lazy; her attitude needs correction.

Therefore important to address during counseling (Raising a child); that the woman is aware of these requirements according to scriptures.

She dedicate the child to the Lord daily

1 Samuel 1:27King James Version (KJV)*27 For this child I prayed; and the Lord hath given me my petition which I asked of him:*

The child is always the best in the mother's eye;

Exodus 2:2King James Version (KJV)*2 And the woman conceived, and bare a son: and when she saw him that he was a goodly child, she hid him three months.*

The mother would do anything for the child, she always does the best for the child. Faced with adversity, Moses' mother had to give him away for his safety.

Hebrews 11:23King James Version (KJV)*23 By faith Moses, when he was born, was hid three months of his parents, because they saw he was a proper child; and they were not afraid of the king's commandment.*

Weaning a child

Genesis 21:8King James Version (KJV)*8 And the child grew, and was weaned: and Abraham made a great feast the same day that Isaac was weaned (*גמל *gimul)*

Note: This Hebrew word translated as "weaned" means to bestow upon, do good, reward. Weaning a child involves speaking blessings and declare having a prosperous life.

Train the child

Proverbs 22:6King James Version (KJV)**6** Train (חנך chanuk) up a child in the way he should go: and when he is old, he will not depart from it.

The Hebrew word חנך chanuk translated as train in this verse also means *dedicate*. At first glance; it looks as if the child is being trained by the adult; that observation is correct but the Hebrew text suggests the manner with which the training is administered. Notice once more the word; חנך chanuk; the last letter is pointed with a "Shewa" ך (the two dots on top of the other). The pointer suggests the gender of the subject of the action; a 2nd person feminine singular indicator.

The mother trains by "dedicating" herself to the child because the Hebrew word is translated as; "dedicate you," or "you dedicate yourself."

Performance indicator would be the amount of time one spends with the child. Watching a video of my sixteen month old grand daughter walking behind her father; he teasingly called out; "bye" with hurried steps. Knowing she could not catch up; she literally threw herself on the ground, not only did he stop, he came to rescue her. At that early age, they know how much dedication their parents have for them.

Proverbs 29:15King James Version (KJV)*15 The rod and reproof give wisdom: but a child left to himself bringeth his mother to shame.*

With Joy She administer Training and care

Psalm 113:9King James Version (KJV)*9 He maketh the barren woman to keep house, and to be a joyful mother of children.*

One of the greatest joy for my mother as mentioned in the preface, was to see her children satisfied. I believe she worked doubly as hard as some of the mothers of today, who excuse themselves from household chores when they return from work.

Children learn, not from what their mother say; but from observing what their mothers do. There is always almost a telepathic understanding between a child and the mother. Proverbs chapter thirty one verse two clarifies the relationship between them; "my son; son of my womb; son of my vow."

Son of my vow presented the idea of a soul tie that sometime the child can tell what the mother wants just by the expression on her face.

Speaking of soul tie between child and mother; I want to address an increase in the concept of grand parents attending to the upbringing of little ones.

I was invited to a lunch, upon arrival I found out that the grandchildren were with them for a week; their parents had to work.

On my way home I could not stop thinking of how the children have been robbed of the opportunity to learn from their parents. I had no doubt the grandparents were great parents to their children. The concern is old age involved in the upbringing of young children. The difference is parents teach with LOVE (strength and affection); grandparents teach with DOTING (excessive fondness and reverence), grandchildren get away with things they normally restricted by their parents. The excessive fondness leads to soul tie with the grandparents denying the mother her entitlement.

Very little mention in the scriptures regarding this issue: but one worth visiting is Jacob and his son Benjamin whom he had when Jacob was very old.

Genesis 44:20King James Version (KJV)
20 And we said unto my lord, We have a father, an old man, and a child of his old age, a little one; and his brother is dead, and he alone is left of his mother, and his father loveth him.

Genesis 44:30King James Version (KJV)
30 Now therefore when I come to thy servant my father, and the lad be not with us; seeing that his life (נפש nephesh) is bound (קשר qashar) up in the lad's life;

נפש nephesh mean soul; קשר qashar means to tie physically, mentally. Jacob testified that he would die should something happen to Benjamin (Genesis 44:31).

I want to especially address the working mothers' duties from the time of conception to teen years.

In Uteri Son of my womb is a confession of the mother according to Proverbs 31:2; Another verse hopefully will substantiate the importance of this stage when the child is still in the mother's womb.

Psalm 139:13King James Version (KJV)13 For thou hast possessed my reins: thou hast *covered me* (סכני sakaniy) in my mother's womb

The Hebrew word סכני **sakaniy** comes from the Hebrew root word סכן sakan meaning to wont, or to become accustomed to, behavior.

I can only suggest that there is scriptural evidence that the home making process starts from the womb. The mother is responsible for ensuring that she always has a joyful attitude. While you are reading this you can think of numerous ideas to enhance the child's growth whilst in the womb.

Behavioral pattern starts from the womb

Psalm 58:3King James Version (KJV) *3 The wicked are estranged (זור* **zuwr**) *from the womb: they go astray as soon as they be born, speaking lies*

זור **zuwr** means to turn aside profane to estrange

Behavior is not the only thing developed in the womb; God ordained and call people in the womb; as found in the fifth verse of Jeremiah chapter one.

Another reference is found in Genesis 25:23; when God told Rebekah, the wife of Isaac that she would have twins. But God did not say twins, he referred to them as "Two Nations." thus their destinies are foretold.

Genesis 25:23King James Version (KJV)*23 And the Lord said unto her, Two nations are in thy womb, and two manner of people shall be separated from thy bowels; and the one people shall be strong-er than the other people; and the elder shall serve the younger.*

FATHER

The Disciplinarian
Ensure comfort for child and mother during pregnancy

Exodus 21:22King James Version (KJV)*22 If men strive, and hurt a woman with child, so that her fruit de-part from her, and yet no mischief follow: he shall be surely punished, according as the woman's husband will lay upon him; and he shall pay as the judges determine*

Fears the Lord

Fearing the Lord is not about being afraid, nor is it about being apprehensive; it's about knowing one is enveloped in the presence of the Lord. In fact wherever one goes the presence follows.

The phrase "presence of the Lord" is the translation of the Hebrew phrase; פני אלהים paney elohiym, face of God.

פני peney means face. Hence presence of the Lord is the face of the Lord. Also to be before the Lord as implemented in Isaiah.

Isaiah 37:14King James Version (KJV)14 And Hezekiah received the letter from the hand of the messengers, and read it: and Hezekiah went up unto the house of the Lord, and spread it before the Lord. (פני יהוה peney adonay)

Exodus 33:14King James Version (KJV)
And he said, My presence (פָּנַי **panay**) shall go with thee, and I will give thee rest.

Speaking to Moses, God is saying that my face will go with you. Where you go, my face will follow.

The knowledge of God's face on you, ensures compliance to His precepts; also a deterrent from mischievous and evil conduct when your Heavenly Father watches you; thus the fear of the Lord.

Proverbs 14:26King James Version (KJV)*26 In the fear of the Lord is strong confidence: and his children shall have a place of refuge*

The children are not interested hearing you when it comes to confidence. They watch and see how you handle situations. According to Proverbs chapter fourteen verse twenty six, strong confidence is nurtured in the fear of the Lord.

Leaves an inheritance for his children's children

Proverbs 13:22King James Version (KJV)*22 A good man leaveth an inheritance to his children's children: and the wealth of the sinner is laid up for the just*

Discipline

Proverbs 23:13King James Version (KJV)*13 Withhold (תמנע timnaʿ) not correction from the child: for if thou beatest him with the rod, he shall not die.*

תמנע timnaʿ is an inflection of the Hebrew verb, מנע mana, meaning withhold. the prefix ת tav indicates the subject as "2ⁿᵈ person masculine singular; you." Discipline that comes from the father includes "not withholding correction."

Proverbs 13:24King James Version (KJV)
24 He that spareth his rod hateth his son: but he that loveth him chasteneth him betimes.

What type of correction?

Correction is translated from the Hebrew word מוסר muwsar meaning; discipline, instruction. A derivative of the verb יסר yasar; meaning to chastise; literally with blows, or figuratively with words. Important to notice the word מוסר muwsar means instruction vital to the discipline process. Children should be explained the reason for discipline; and to some degree informed of the yield of fruit of righteousness.

Hebrews 12:11King James Version (KJV)
11 Now no chastening for the present seemeth to be joyous, but grievous: nevertheless afterward it yieldeth the peaceable fruit of righteousness unto them which are exercised thereby.

Man of integrity

Proverbs 20:7 King James Version (KJV) 7 *The just man walketh in his integrity: his children are blessed after him*

As weight is measured in grams; integrity is measured in righteousness. The man's word balances with righteousness, his deeds balances with righteousness, his relationship with God and his neighbor balances with righteousness.

Job 31:6 King James Version (KJV)
6 Let me be weighed in an even balance that God may know mine integrity.

Note: Every man should be mindful of the fact; his input and how he conducts himself will influence the blessings bestowed for his generation to come.

References

Dr Michael Brown
https://stream.org/yes-childhood-sexual-abuse-often-contribute-homosexuality/

Poverty
Source: World Bank, Development Research Group (2009) http://www.un.org/esa/socdev/rwss/docs/2010/chapter2.pdf

United Nation http://www.un.org/sustainabledevelopment/

Raising Children Network http://raisingchildren.net.au/articles/child_development.html

Emotional Trauma in the Womb By Samuel López De Victoria, Ph.D. ttps://psychcentral.com/blog/archives/2010/06/29/emotional-trauma-in-the-womb/

Janice Mac Avoy
http://www.smh.com.au/comment/im-a-successful-lawyer-and-mother-because-i-had-an-abortion-20160124-gmd81d.html

Health Line
https://www.healthline.com/health/pregnancy/when-can-a-fetus-hear#1

Acknowledgement

First I want to give honor and praise to God my creator for the breath of life, protection and the leading of His Holy Spirit.

My siblings, their families and friends speaking good things into my life.

Many I may not name who contributed to who I am today, I want to acknowledge your sacrifices. My two children Varitema and Gilbert, you are always in my heart.

The Whippy family in Sydney, for putting up with me the last few years; my prayer you have long lives to witness the many blessings my heavenly Father bring your way.

Members of Central Messianic One New Man; few but strong. Thank you for your prayers and support.

Fellow pastors and their families; Rev Qele Ratu; Senior Pastor Lighthouse Family Worship Centre. Rev Mikaele Modrau; founder– BGPT Equipping Ministry, Pastor Joseva Rokobatini; Senior Pastor Gracefield Community Church.

Central Messianic One New Man (Fiji Ministry) Immanuel and Hallelujah Chesed - thank you and the members of your family, I am honored to be called your friend.

Last but not least my eldest sister Amelia Talakicau Tagi, thank you for trusting me.

Pastor Elisha-Rei Jacobs

Pastor Central Messianic One New Man (Central Christian Fellowship, Australian Christian Churches.)

Born, Aminio Vakatalesau Modrau to Jone and Irinieta Modrau, in a little village in Fiji called Tumavia, province of Tailevu. Moved to Australia in 1987 after the first Military coup in search for greener pastures. Five years earlier, his marriage ended after 6 years, 5 month and 3 weeks. Had two children; Varitema and Gilbert, but never married again.

Changed his name to Elisha-Rei Jacobs 2009 through revelations in regard to the mantle of the "former name" as a false prophet in the old Fijian Cultic Worship.

Studied Hebrew with "HEBREW UNIVERSITY OF JERUSALEM – ONLINE ACADEMY"

Passionate in sharing the accurate knowledge in the Word of God.

Now an Australian citizen and lives in Sydney